# GERMANY AND AMERICA 1450–1700

Julius Friedrich Sachse's
*History of the
German Role in the Discovery, Exploration,
and Settlement of the New World*

Edited by *Don Heinrich Tolzmann*

HERITAGE BOOKS
2015

## HERITAGE BOOKS
*AN IMPRINT OF HERITAGE BOOKS, INC.*

### Books, CDs, and more—Worldwide

For our listing of thousands of titles see our website
at
www.HeritageBooks.com

Published 2015 by
HERITAGE BOOKS, INC.
Publishing Division
5810 Ruatan Street
Berwyn Heights, Md. 20740

Copyright © 1991 Don Heinrich Tolzmann

All rights reserved. No part of this book may be reproduced or transmitted in any form or by any means, electronic or mechanical, including photocopying, recording or by any information storage and retrieval system without written permission from the author, except for the inclusion of brief quotations in a review.

International Standard Book Numbers
Paperbound: 978-1-55613-539-2
Clothbound: 978-0-7884-6179-8

## TABLE OF CONTENTS

PREFACE . . . . . . . . . . v

PART ONE - EDITOR'S COMMENTS . . . . . . 1
   Introduction . . . . . . . . . . 3
   The Life and Work of Julius Friedrich Sachse . . . . . 5
   German-American Studies, 1492-1992 and Beyond . . . . 16

PART TWO - SACHSE'S HISTORY . . . . . . . 31
   Historical Introduction . . . . . . . . 33
   At the Close of the Medieval Era . . . . . . . 42
   Dawn of the Modern Period . . . . . . . . 63
   Effect of the Great Discoveries . . . . . . . 71
   The Earliest Attempt at German Colonization . . . . . 81
   The Store of Welserland . . . . . . . . 95
   The Grants to Anton and Hieronymus Fugger . . . . . 107
   Religious Causes Inducive to German Emigration. . . . . 115
   The Thirty Years War . . . . . . . . 122
   Dutch and Swedish Attempts at Colonization . . . . . 132
   The French Wars of Conquest . . . . . . . 140
   German Emigration to America . . . . . . . 169
   Literature Used to Induce German Emigration . . . . . 175
   Appendix . . . . . . . . . . 199

PART THREE - EDITOR'S CONCLUSION . . . . . 259
   Conclusion . . . . . . . . . . 261
   Sources for Further Study . . . . . . . . 262

WORKS BY THE EDITOR . . . . . . . . 265

## PREFACE

1992 marks the year of a worldwide celebration - the 500th anniversary of the discovery/re-discovery of America by Columbus. The purpose of this work is to provide a German-American contribution to this event by making Julius Friedrich Sachse's history of the German role in the discovery, exploration, and early settlement of the New World again available as a new edition. Originally published in 1897, this history first appeared in the annual proceedings of the Pennsylvania German Society. After I wrote to the Society requesting permission to prepare a new edition of this work, the Society's Editor, the Rev. Frederick S. Weiser, informed me that the work was no longer covered by copyright, so that he could not grant "permission," but would rather offer a "blessing" instead. I, therefore, would like to express gratitude to the Pennsylvania German Society for their encouragement in the undertaking of the preparation of this new edition of Sachse's work for the 500th anniversary of the discovery of America.

In the course of time, this has proved to be a valuable and basic source of information for all those interested in the German dimension as it relates to America in the period from 1450 to 1700. It originally appeared after the 1892 celebration of the 400th anniversary of the discovery of America, but has long been unavailable and inaccessible. The advent of the 1992 anniversary appeared to be the appropriate time to make this work available once again, especially because of the importance of German-American relations internationally, as well as because of the renewed interest in the German heritage.

Don Heinrich Tolzmann<br>
University of Cincinnati

PART ONE - EDITOR'S COMMENTS

## Introduction

This work originally appeared with the following title: *The Fatherland (1450-1700)*...The editor felt that a more appropriate title was: *Germany and America (1450-1700)*...as this more accurately describes that the book is dealing with the earliest contacts between the two countries.

This work is divided into three parts. In Part One the editor has provided a biographical essay dealing with the life and work of Julius Friedrich Sachse. This is followed by an essay especially written for the 500th anniversary of the discovery of America, which traces, outlines, and discusses five centuries of German life in America, as well as the development of the field of German-American Studies. In Part Two we find the work of Sachse, which is followed by Part Three. This contains concluding comments of the editor together with a list of sources for further reading and study.

# The Life and Work of Julius Friedrich Sachse

## Introduction

In the several decades before the First World War, the field of German-American Studies blossomed as never before. (1) In 1883 the German-American Bicentennial, the celebration of the establishment of the first permanent German settlement at Germantown, Pennsylvania, in 1683, had taken place, and by the late 1890s the date of this celebration, the 6th of October, had become a widely celebrated festivity known simply as "German Day." (2) It was also in the latter decades of the nineteenth century that a number of regional German-American historical and heritage societies were formed, such as the Society for the History of the Germans in Maryland and the Pennsylvania German Society. In the early 1900s the German-American Historical Society was formed, providing a national focus to many of the regional studies which were being done. (3)

One of the major German-American historians a century ago was, without question, Dr. Julius Fredrich Sachse. (4) An indication of his stature was the fact that he attained biographical listings in major reference sources, such as *Who's Who in America* and *Dictionary of American Biography*. (5) His standing in the field of German-Amerian Studies, especially in his area of specialization, Pennsylvania German Studies, was high. An obituary from the annual proceedings of the Pennsylvania German Society stated "Dr. Sachse ranked among the foremost of our historians." (6) Indeed, it was felt that he had "a greater influence from anyone else on the quality" of the publications of the Society from the 1890s until his death in 1919. (7) Moreover, his demise was "probably the greatest loss which the Pennsylvania German Society has sustained at any time..." (8)

Sachse focussed especially on the early periods of German-American history, and "what he wrote, as the result of extensive research, has become the standard authority on the subject." (9) Today, his works continue to be reprinted, and his works are cited in all the standard bibliographies in the field of German-American Studies. (10)

## The Life of Sachse

Sachse was born 22 November 1842 in Philadelphia as the son of German immigrants, Johann Heinrich Friedrich and Julianna Wilhelmina (Buehler) Sachse. His father was an artist and designer with bronze and other metals, who had studied with Bertel Thorwaldsen, the Danish sculptor. (11) This artistic family background would later find expression in the beautifully illustrated works of Sachse.

Educated in the grammar schools of Philadelphia, and later in the old Lutheran Academy, Sachse then became a haberdasher and manufacturer of men's shirts. At several fairs in Vienna he received medals for the works he had produced. On 15 May 1864 he married a German-American named Emma Caroline Lange, and together they would have five children. After a prosperous business career in the years after the Civil War, he retired in 1890 at the rather early age of forty-eight, so that he could devote himself to photography and German-American historical research. Here we see the combination of his two major areas of interest: history and photography, the latter reflecting the artistic orientation of his family, and the former his special interest.

As a photographer he freelanced for *The American Journal of Photography*, *The Ladies' Home Journal*, and for several book publishers. His photography was noted for its exceptional beauty and high quality, and one of his major works was a series of studies which were produced in his own hothouse, of the development of the Cereus, which blossoms only at night. His artistic work with photography had a direct impact and influence on his books, in that they all were "lavishly embellished with photographs, zincographic facsimiles, and pen and ink drawings," which Sachse all prepared with great care and skill. (12)

Because of his interest in history and research, Sachse joined a number of organizations and societies related to this interest. However, as a German-American in Pennsylvania, his major interest would be for the Pennsylvania German heritage, and this would take form in the role he played in the establishment of the Pennsylvania German Society. (13)

In 1891 he became one of the founders of the Society. He served as Treasurer for twenty-three years (from 1891 to 1913), as President (from 1913 to 1914), and then as a member of the Executive Committee until his death in 1919. In his presidential address in Lancaster, Pennsylvania, before the Society on 13 November 1914 he noted:

"It is just twenty-four years ago. It was in November 1890, when the late Dr. W.H. Egle, the State Librarian at Harrisburg, consulted with me, at a meeting of the Pennsylvania Historical Society at Philadelphia, upon the advisability of forming a patriotic hereditary society from the descendants of the early German and Swiss emigrants to Pennsylvania upon the same lines as the lately formed Society to the Sons of the Revolution, from which so many Pennsylvania-Germans (only those without an ancestor in the Revolution) were debarred, as it was their ancestors who had helped to feed and clothe the patriot army, but had not given any military service." (14)

On 26 February 1891 a little group met in the study of Dr. J. Max Hark's Moravian parsonage at Lancaster. Here the group made plans for the formation of the new society, "which has since attained such an enviable standing in its efforts to give publicity to the great deeds and work of the early German and Swiss immigrants to this country, with their bearing upon the development which it has since attained." (15)

At the organizational meeting of 15 April 1891 held at the Lancaster Court House, Sachse was elected Treasurer. His service as one of the founding fathers was obviously basic to the establishment of the Pennsylvania German Society. Upon his death, it was said that the Society had sustained "the greatest loss...at any time" in its history to that point. (16) In all of his years of service, he had approached his work with his accustomed zeal. (17) Samuel Pennypacker later wrote of the Society that, "No other of the different race societies has been so energetic in the study of the sources of history or so prolific in the production of literature." (18) And it was Sachse who, without question, contributed to this reputation enjoyed by the Society.

In the first twenty-five years of the Pennsylvania German Society, Sachse was one of the three guiding forces, along with Frank Reid Diffenderfer and Henry Melchoir Muhlenberg Richards. (19) According to a Pennsylvania German history, "these men worked indefatigably in behalf of the Society and the preservation of Pennsylvania German history." (20) Indeed, the three became the major pillars of the Society, so that they have been referred to as "the Triumvirate." (21)

The advent of the First World War placed the German element in a difficult position. Just as Anglo-America was pro-English in the neutrality period, so, too was German-America pro-German. (22) After Wilson obtained a declaration of war against Germany in 1917, a tragic display of anti-German hysteria swept the land, affecting all Americans of German ancestry. (23) Even though the

Pennsylvania Germans had already been in America for many generations, they, too, faced the brunt of the anti-German hysteria. At that time, most German-Americans felt placed in the situation of being forced to stress their patriotism, or to attempt to demonstrate and prove their Americanism, so as to escape being the target of the anti-Germans. (24)

The war "brought dark days for the Pennsylvania Germans. They thought they were under suspicion of being pro-German." (25) In his 1914 presidential address to the Society which took place shortly after the war's outbreak on 13 November, Sachse took pains to point out the Americanism of the Pennsylvania Germans, as he stated that "this organization is strictly a Native American organization with no entanglement with any foreign power." (26) Sachse's address itself is an important historical document of the situation of the German-American at the time. He stated:

"We are not less Americans because our ancestors came from the German Fatherland over 115 years ago, to these western wilds, settled here; cleared the forests, and turned the wilderness into fertile fields, suffered under the incursions of the savages, who were incited to fury by the French and English, and later fought for independence of their adopted country, and were important factors in establishing the American government under the present constitution." (27)

Sachse then went on in his address to point out that it was Frederick Augustus Muehlenberg, a Pennsylvania German, who became the first Speaker of the House of Representatives, and that two Pennsylvania Germans were in the Hall of Fame in Washington, D.C. He pointed out also that even though some of the German-American settlers were by religious faith opposed to the bearing of arms, that this "did not forbid them from nursing the sick and wounded soldiers back to health, or if they died, giving them a Christian burial...Then again it was these very German settlers and their children who clothed and fed the American army during the critical period while they were in winter quarters upon the bleak hillsides at Valley Forge in the Memorable Winter of 1777-1778." He notes that the German counties of Pennsylvania became the "granaries of the American army, whenever the tide of the conflict surged to this vicinity." Sachse then cites Bancroft who wrote, "Neither they nor their descendants have laid claim to all that is their due." Sachse comments that, "They have permitted their more aggressive neighbors to deny them a proper place even on the historical page." (28)

Commenting on the Pennsylvania German Society, Sachse states that, "It is the aim and privilege of the Pennsylvania German Society to controvert the slanders so ruthlessly made against the race, and place it in its proper light before the community at large." He asked how could one know anything of American history without a knowledge of the role of the German-American? (29)

It is a tribute to Sachse that the strategy of placing an emphasis on the Americanism of the Society effectively brought the Pennsylvania Germans through a tragic period in German-American history. As noted earlier, Sachse continued to serve the Society until his death in 1919, fortunately surviving the war by a year.

Before turning to his work, a word is in order about Sachse, the person. He was noted for his "unflagging enthusiasm" and "much of his influence was due to his engaging personal qualities." (30) He was described as a self-made man who was "in many respects...a remarkable man." (31) Sachse was "a fine example of the strong mind in a strong body, which, with his active temperament, made him a person of unremitting industry, patient and painstaking in research, especially in the procuring of original matter." (32) Members of the Pennsylvana German Society considered him "an ever true and sincere friend, one who was always a Christian gentleman." (33) According to Rosenberger, Sachse "had an outgoing personality and a modest manner that won many friends." (34)

## The Work of Sachse

The publications of Sachse can be divided into two subject areas: those dealing with German-American history and those dealing with Masonic history. (35) The latter was his major research interest after German-Americana. Sachse served from 1906 until his death as the Librarian and Curator of the Grand Lodge of F. & A.M. of Pennsylvania, and he was a prominent member of various Masonic bodies. It is, therefore, not surprising that he wrote a number of works dealing with the history of Masonry: *Freemasonry in Pennsylvania, 1727-1907*; *Old Masonic Lodges of Pennsylvania, Modern and Ancient, 1730-1800*; *Bi-Centennial of the Birth of Right Worshipful Past Grand Master Brother Benjamin Franklin*; and *Washington's Masonic Correspondence as Found in the Washington Papers in the Library of Congress*. Many of these works shed interesting light on the eighteenth century, especially with regard to Franklin and Washington. However, the major focal point of Sachse's research and publication would be in the area of the German heritage.

His first publication in the field of German-American Studies was the volume edited here for publication. It appeared in 1897 in the annual proceedings of the Pennsylvania German Society. At the time, it was considered a work "of the highest order, beautifully and profusely illustrated, which met universal appreciation and gave an impetus and standing to the entire undertaking which has been sustained ever since." (36) His following works continued this excellence and Sachse also "continued to embellish them with copious and most excellent illustrations, many of them original, others copies of rare historic pictures." (37)

Altogether, thirty-four publications are listed of Sachse's which deal with German-American history. (38) These range from essay-length studies to major and substantial monographs. In recognition of his numerous scholarly publications, the degree of Doctor of Letters (Litt.D.) was conferred on him in 1900 by the Muhlenberg College. A special area of interest for him was the pre-1800 period in German-American history, which meant of course, that many of his works focussed on the Pennsylvania German experience. One of his major works in this area appeared in 1899: *The German Sectarians of Pennsylvania, 1708-1742: A Critical and Legendary History of the Ephrata Cloister and the Dunkers*. Recently reprinted in 1971, this has become the standard source on the topic. Sachse noted in the foreword that his sole aim was "to tell the true story...of the German influence in the settlement and development" of Pennsylvania, and that this work focussed on one particular aspect of German-American religious history. (39)

According to the *Dictionary of American Biography*, the "chief merits of his historical work were his unflagging enthusiasm and his faculty for discovering materials." (40) It should be noted that he was basically a self-educated and trained scholar, but, nevertheless, his works did "more than the writings of anyone else to awaken interest in Pennsylvania German history." (41) Among the more than two dozen works in the field of German-American history, the present work, edited here for re-publication, is one that has stood the test of time. Perhaps the best evaluation of his work was that of Henry Melchior Muhlenberg Richards, who wrote:

"As an annalist, biographer, compiler, collector, and as a practical illustrator, along the lines of the specialties of his study and research, he was unsurpassed and has left behind him voluminous and striking evidences of his faithful and comprehensive labors in his chosen field of investigation. He took an absorbing interest in all historical movements and organizations in Pennsylvania and was an important factor in their establishment and perpetuation." (42)

Notes:

1. See Don Heinrich Tolzmann, "German-American Studies: History and Development," *Monatshefte*, 80:3(1988): 278-88.

2. With regard to the German Day celebration, see Don Heinrich Tolzmann, *In der Neuen Heimat: Deutsch-Amerikanische Festschrift fuer die 500-Jahrfeier der Entdeckung von Amerika*, (New York: Peter Lang Pub. Co., 1992).

3. See John Appel, "Marion Dexter Learned and the German-American Historical Society," *Pennsylvania Magazine for History and Biography*, 86(1962):287-318.

4. For references to German-American scholars, see Don Heinrich Tolzmann, *German-Americana: A Bibliography*, (Metuchen, New Jersey: Scarecrow Pr., 1975), pp. 242-44.

5. See *Who Was Who in America: A Companion Volume to Who's Who in America: Volume 1, 1897-1942*, (Chicago: Marquis, 1943), p. 1072; and *Dictionary of American Biography*, (New York: Scribner, 1935), vol. 16, p. 282.

6. Henry Melchior Muhlenberg Richards, "Julius Friedrich Sachse, Litt. D.," *Pennsylvania German Society Proceedings*, 31(1925): 43.

7. Richards, p. 40.

8. Richards, p. 43.

9. Richards, p. 43.

10. See Tolzmann, *German-Americana: A Bibliography*.

11. See Bertel Thorwaldsen, *Thorwaldsen*, (Berlin: Weise, 1938).

12. *Dictionary of American Biography*, p. 282.

13. With regard to the 1991 centennial celebration of the Pennsylvania German Society, see "Publications of the Pennsylvania German Society and its Predecessors, 1891-1991," *Der Reggeboge*, 25:1(1991):1-32.

14. Homer T. Rosenberger, *The Pennsylvania Germans, 1891-1965*, (Lancaster, Pa.: Pennsylvania German Society, 1966), p. 74.

15. Rosenberger, p. 73.

16. Richards, p. 40.

17. Rosenberger, p. 97.

18. Rosenberger, p. 73.

19. Rosenberger, pp. 101-103.

20. Rosenberger, p. 101.

21. Rosenberger, p. 101.

22. With regard to World War One, see LaVern J. Rippley, *The German-Americans*, (Boston: Twayne, 1976).

23. See Frederick Luebke, *Bonds of Loyalty: German-Americans and World War I*, (Dekalb: Northern Illinois University, 1974).

24. See Carl Wittke, *German-Americans and the World War: With Special Emphasis on Ohio's German-language Press*, (Columbus: Ohio Historical Society, 1936).

25. Rosenberger, p. 129.

26. Rosenberger, p. 129.

27. See the *Pennsylvania German Society Proceedings*, 25(1914): 18.

28. *Proceedings*, pp. 18-19.

29. *Proceedings*, pp. 21.

30. *Dictionary of American Biography*, p. 282.

31. Richards, p. 45.

32. Richards, p. 45.

33. Richards, p. 46.

34. Rosenberger, p. 103.

35. For an overview of his Masonic historical works, see Richards, pp. 43.-44.

36. Richards, p. 41.

37. Richards, p. 41.

38. See Henry A. Pochmann, *Bibliography of German Culture in America to 1940*, (Madison: University of Wisconsin, 1953), pp. 309-10.

39. See Julius Friedrich Sachse, *The German Sectarians of Pennsylvania*...(1899; rpt.: New York: AMS Pr, 1971), p. viii.

40. *Dictionary of American Biography*, p. 282.

41. *Ibid.*

42. Richards, p. 45.

## German-American Studies, 1492-1992 and Beyond

### Introduction:

In 1492 the world stood at the threshhold of a new era - an era that forever altered the course of history - America was discovered. And ever since that time the New World has dominated the imagination of mankind, and especially that of the German-speaking world. For example, Paul Baginsky's bibliography of German works dealing with America lists 1,600 publications for the 308 years from 1493 to 1800, or an average of 519 works per year. (1) Germans were fascinated with the Americas. It became the ideal, hope, and the dream of those in the Old World who in some way, were dissatisfied with the social, political, economic, or religious conditions of their homelands. The New World would become the destination point of millions in the greatest world-wide population movement in the history of the planet. Approximately ten million German-speaking people from every corner of Europe became part of this global *Voelkerwanderung*, and would come to the New World, to both North and South America. They came to establish a new life and home for themselves, their families, and children, and their descendants. Some were exiles and hoped to return, but most came with the intention of permanently establishing a new home. Today the German elements in both North and South America surpass in number the populations of the German-speaking ancestral homelands in Europe.

In the history of this five century-long global immigration movement, the German immigrations represent, without question, a major chapter. It is well to keep this global perspective in mind, since Germans immigrated not only to the Americas, but elsewhere around the world. They not only moved west to the Americas, but in Europe they settled the southeastern provinces of the old Austro-Hungarian Empire, and they settled in large numbers in Russia. While it is not unusual for a German family to have branches in Russia and in the Americas, the bulk of the German immigration was to the Americas, not to the European southeast and east. The descendants of many of those who did move to the southeast and east have now found their way, as a result of the world wars, back to Germany, and some have found their way to the New World. The German immigrations, in short, are a basic part of world history, and an essential part of the histories of the various countries in the western hemisphere. The Americas became, in the course of five centuries, the western frontier of the German-speaking countries of Europe, and are closely tied together by this basic familial interrelationship.

The history of the German immigrations and the Old and New World interrelationship are, hence, of major importance for a history of the Americas. The study and research of this topic is not only of academic interest, it is essential for an understanding of American and European history, as well as that of the local German-American communities, and how they are both ultimately and inextricably interrelated.

What does this all mean? What does it mean that tens of millions of German-speaking people left their homelands to come to the New World in the course of the last five centuries? This requires an understanding of European history, as well as that of the New World. If you do not understand the immigrations to America, you cannot understand the Americas, because they are, in essence, nations composed of immigrants and their descendants. Their past history, their contemporary heritage, and their future cultural development are integral parts of the national histories of the countries where they have settled. They are also of significance for world history since 1492, and also for contemporary and future international relations. The German dimension plays a vital role with regard to questions pertaining to the past, present, and future in the Americas. What then is the task of German-American Studies in this regard?

German-American Studies:

German-American Studies can be defined as the scholarly study, research, and teaching of the history, language, literature, and culture of the German elements in the Americas. This includes coverage of the immigrants and their offspring from Germany, Austria, and Switzerland, and other German-speaking areas of Europe, especially Russia. Several points require further elaboration here.

First, the term "German" is used here in a linguistic, cultural, and ethnic sense to cover the totality of the German-speaking immigrants and their descendants. It is, therefore, not confined to the states which in 1870-71 were united in the German Empire. Indeed, one-fourth of the German-speaking immigrants came from other states and regions of Europe. In some regions of the Americas, the German element may be from one of these regions outside of Germany.

Second, the term "German-American Studies" refers to the field of study, research, and teaching which spans an entire hemisphere, from North to South. In fact, however, the field subdivides into North and South American divisions. In the North, German-Canadian and German-American Studies in the U.S., form the sub-branches. In South America, the situation is more complex, where the German elements in 17 states and regions have been identified. Although closely interrelated, the North and South American divisions have, in fact, developed separately and on their own. For example, each sub-branch needs to be approached with special attention to its own particular socio-cultural context and historical development.

Because of the various pressing pragmatic concerns amongst scholars within the various sub-branches, there have been few attempts at a hemispheric approach in the field. Such an approach is appropriate at this time in the development of the field, and would be mutually beneficial for all those interested in the German heritage. There are already precedents for such an approach. Already in the 19th century *Der Deutsche Pionier*, an historical journal published in Cincinnati, contained articles and essays on the German-Canadians, German-Amerians, and German-Brazilians, etc. (2) Karl J.R. Arndt is well known for his magisterial *Die deutschsprachige Presse der Amerikas*, which records German-language newspapers and their library holdings across the hemisphere. Hartmut Froeschle of Toronto is also well known for his work on the Germans in South America and the U.S., aside from his major contributions to German-Canadian Studies. (3) These pioneers pointed the way which needs to be emulated in the future. The purpose of this essay is to provide a general overview of the development of the field of German-American Studies, so as to provide guidance with regard to how the field has developed, and with regard to how it may develop in the future.

Since this field is of necessity closely interwoven with the history of the Germans in the New World, we need to first examine the last five centuries with regard to the history of the Germans in the Americas. These past five centuries can be divided into five basic historical periods, and in in each some basic characteristics can be identified.

### 1. The Age of Discovery:

#### Basic Characteristics

What can be said of the basic characteristics of the German involvement in the discovery of the New World? It has been often noted that in the struggle for the Americas the Latin nations sent officers without an army, the English, both officers and an army, the Germans, an army without officers. This pertains to the fact that the absence of a united German homeland rendered state-sponsored exploration an impossibility, but that Germans were to be found in the explorations sponsored especially by the Latin nations. One can find many examples of Germans as explorers, adventurers, missionaries, mercenaries, etc.

## Basic Facts

Although the discovery of America is associated with Columbus and 1492, there is the old Norse legend that the first German in America was Tyrker, who was a member of the Norse expedition of Leif Ericson which attempted to settle somewhere between Labrador and New England. These legends and sagas need further investigation, as do other pre-Columbian contacts to America.

Although not directly involved in the 1492 discovery/re-discovery, Germans played the major role in the dissemination of information regarding this event, since Germans were predominant in the art, industry, and trade of printing after moveable type was invented in the Rhineland in the 1440s. Across Europe, printing presses were usually not without German printers. And so in 1493 Stefan Planck in Rome printed the letter of Columbus, which was called a little book, or pamphlet, since it consisted of a few pages. This became the first publication about America. It found its way to Anton Koberger in Nuremberg who included it in his 1497 edition of the *Nuremberg Chronicle*, the first actual book to mention the recent discovery. The Columbus letter was printed across Europe by German printers, and was perhaps the first real best-seller. It told of "gold and pearls in the islands, treasures that would one day dwarf those of Solomon." In the next few years German presses worked overtime to supply the great need for information about the newly found land as "the whole of Europe seemed to be fevered by the idea of Utopia, a dream of earthly paradise." In 1498 Sebastian Brant mentioned the discovery in his *Narrenschiff* which was published in 1509 as *The Ship of Fools*, the first English-language publication to cite the 1492 event. Therefore, with regard to the first publications about the Columbian discovery, Germans played the major role. (5)

A few other basic facts might be mentioned. In 1507, Martin Waldseemueller gave the newly found land the name of "America" based on reports of the new world by Amerigo Vespucci, an Italian sailor in the service of the Portuguese, and placed this new name on his map that he produced that year. A German mapmaker, therefore, gave America its name. In 1519 Jakob Cromberger, a German printer in Seville, printed the first geographical book about America, *Summa de geographia*. The many German works dealing with America which have been published since 1493 can be found in the aforementioned bibliography of Paul Baginsky. One of the many which aroused great interest was the book by Hans Staden, a mercenary from Hessen, who traveled twice to Brazil in the service of the Spanish and the Portuguese, and published his book entitled *Wahrhaftige Geschichte...*, which was published in English as *The Cannibal Book...* This described in detail the customs, religion, food, drink, and culture, as well as the cannibalism of the natives Staden encountered in the New World.

## 2. The First Germans:

### Basic Characteristics

A little more than a quarter century after 1492, one finds the first Germans already in America. With the first Germans we are speaking of individuals who came as explorers, adventurers, soldiers, craftsmen, or churchmen connected with voyages and explorations sponsored mainly by the Latin nations. It is important to note their presence as they would be the first Germans in America. Many of the sub-branches of the field of German-American Studies begin their histories with the establishment of the first German settlements in their respective countries, and often overlook the arrival of the first Germans as the actual starting-point in the history of the German element in a particular country. It is with them that their history should really begin, rather than with the establishment of the first permanent settlement.

### Basic Facts

In South America the first Germans were miners in Santo Domingo who came in 1525, a mere 32 years after Columbus. In the area which became the U.S., Germans first came in 1562 to Port Royal, South Carolina, and in 1664 the first German arrived in Canada. Therefore, from 1525 to 1664, the first Germans had arrived in the Americas. (6)

## 3. Immigration and Settlement:

### Basic Characteristics

After the arrival of the first Germans, the first group immigrations began in the 17th century, which would eventually develop into massive waves. In spite of the absence of German state-sponsored immigration and colonization, German group immigrations were organized so that numerous all-German settlements were established, and it is relatively easy to locate districts, regions, and states where the German immigration concentrated so that the German element is the predominant element there today. German geographical place-names testify to this impact. This period of the great waves of immigration comes to a close with the outbreak of the First World War, which in effect closed the gates abruptly.

This period of immigration and settlement became the Golden Age of the German element with the establishment and flourishing of German institutions such as the church, press, and numerous secular organizations. Also in its early stages of development and evolution was the New World German heritage, a synthesis of both the Old and the New Worlds, be it German-Canadian, German-American, German-Brazilian, etc.

Basic Facts

In 1683 group immigration began to what is now the U.S. when the ship *Concord* arrived with 13 German families who established Germantown, Pennsylvania. In 1750 group immigration to Canada began with the arrival of Germans on the ship *Anne* bound for Halifax. German group immigration to South America began with the establishment of Leopoldina, Brazil, in 1818. This, again, was the period of the major waves of immigration and the establishment of the major institutions associated with the German heritage in the New World. (7)

4. The World Wars:

Basic Characteristics

Following hard on the heels of the so-called Golden Age was the anti-German hysteria of the First World War. This period brought trial, tribulation, and tragedy. The German elements became the targets of persecution across the hemisphere, and there was a concerted effort made to eliminate anything even in the most remote manner associated with the German heritage. This was followed two decades later by another world war, which brought with it, if not the hysteria, a great deal of harassment and suppression of things German, as well as the internment of innocent German-Americans in the U.S.

Basic Facts

The world wars period dates from the outbreak of the First World War until 1960, when this period can be said to have come to a close. A few representative, and in some cases, symbolic events will be cited here.

By the end of the First World War, Berlin, Ontario, Canada had "lost its pride in traditional Germanness, German instruction in public schools, any substantial ethnic leadership by its German-born clergymen, its last German-language newspaper, and even its German name." In 1917 after Brazil broke diplomatic relations with Germany, three days of rioting took place in Porto Allegre which resulted in the destruction of several hundred homes, factories, warehouses, restaurants, schools, newspaper offices, and buildings which belonged to German-Brazilians. Several months later, after the Brazilian declaration of war against Germany, another series of riots resulted in more violence and destruction in the German-Brazilian districts. In 1918, in one of the most despicable acts of the anti-German hysteria, a German-American, falsely accused of being a spy, was lynched at Collinsville, Illinois. (8)

As a result of the world wars, renewed immigration took place in the interwar period, as well as after the Second World War. After the First there was renewed immigration with the dissolution of the German and the Austro-Hungarian Empires, which was followed in the Thirties with the arrival of the exiles across the Americas. The 1950s brought with them the arrival of Germans expelled from their ancestral homelands in eastern Germany, in central and southeastern Europe, and in Russia. These waves of immigrants, whose motivations for leaving their homelands occureed under tragic circumstances, had by and large a most definite and positive influence on New World German elements, many of which had been extremely demoralized by the pervasive anti-German Zeitgeist of the world wars. The new arrivals, many of whom had been ethnic Germans who lived outside of Germany but had preserved their ethnicity, worked as an antidote with their strong desire and enthusiasm for their heritage. Therefore, in spite of the tragic aspects of this period, the arrival of the new immigrants brings this period to a hopeful conclusion.

5. From Ethnic Survival to Ethnic Revival:

If the preceding period can be described as one where the central concern was one of ethnic survival for Germans as an ethnic group, then the following and present period may be described as one of ethnic revival, and one which began in the 1960s. In the U.S. there occurred what has been called the ethnic revival, which resulted in the public and official legitimization of ethnicity as a permanent factor in American society. In 1965 the Elementary and Secondary Education Act referred to the U.S. as a "multiethnic society" and the 1972 Ethnic Heritage Studies Act, according to its proponents, aimed to begin "a new federal effort to legitimate ethnicity and pluralism in America." One of its sponsors claimed that the act gave "official recognition to ethnicity as a positive constructive force" in American society. (9)

In Canada in 1971, Prime Minister Trudeau announced Canada's "official policy of implementing Multiculturalism within a bilingual framework." According to the Minister of State Responsible for Multiculturalism, this concept "is nothing less than a recognition of the right of every Canadian to maintain his heritage and a repudiation of the melting-pot concept." (10) Especially important for the development of German-American Studies was the establishment of new organizations, such as the Society for German-American Studies (1968) and the German Canadian Historical Association (1973).

German-American Studies:

The development of German-American Studies roughly parallels the history of the German element in the Americas. The development of the field in North and South followed these general patterns:

1. The Church History Period:

This period began in the colonial era, and its sources are the published and unpublished writings of church officials, missionaries, clergymen, and adventurers who came to the New World. These writings include religious histories, journals, diaries, biographies, autobiographies, and all types of church records and document. All of these materials provided not only the early image of the New World, but the foundations for the historical understanding and reflection of the group experience of the German element. (11)

2. The Pioneer Period:

This period began in the mid-nineteenth century and came to a close by the end of the century. The pioneer were not professional scholars, of course, but rather businessmen, journalists, and politicians who had an interest in recording their own experiences, as well as those of their own communities.They produced, for the first time, histories of their communities in the German langauage. They also succeeded in uncovering and preserving a great number of valuable primary souce materials, which were largely ignored by the non-German historians of their respective countries. A valuable journal of this period was, for example, *Der Deutsche Pionier*, which chronicled the history of the German heritage in the Americas. Amateur historians of this period recognized that their basic task was to collect and to preserve information and sources for later generations. Heinrich

A. Rattermann, for example, who edited the aforementioned journal, stated that his task "was that of searching, collecting, and investigating," but he also noted that he was not a trained scholar with the appropriate education to construct a scholarly historical work. He said that he "possessed the talent to solve, explain, and develop, but not the readiness to assimilate the material into a coordinated form." This, of course, was so, because the pioneers were not trained scholars and historians, but rather part-time amateurs, with some exceptional standards. (12)

### 3. Filiopietism:

This period began in the late 19th century, extended down to the First World War, and was characterized by an overemphasis on the oustanding contributions made by the German element. Here we see the reaction of those of German origin to the fact that their history and accomplishments were largely excluded from the standard histories of their New World homelands. To counter this they stressed the outstanding contributions members of their communities had made, and they began to publish their works in the language of their respective countries. They did so in an attempt to reach the historians and scholars who did not understand the German language, as well as to reach out to the American-born generations. By this approach they were beginning to make some actual inroads into academia before the First World War, and also attracting to their field of study those of non-German origin. This was an indication that the field was becoming accepted as an academic field of study and research. Many of these fine efforts were brought to an abrupt and harsh close by the advent of the First World War, after which time few proclaimed the contributions made by the German element.

### 4. German-American Studies during the World War Period:

In the war period, a small number of scholars continued their work in the field of German-American Studies. Their work was devoid of the filiopietism of the earlier period, and was characterized by the highest standards of objectivity and academic quality. The number of those involved was small; nevertheless they helped lay the foundation for the rapid expansion of the field since the 1960s.

### 5. The Ethnic Revival:

Since the 1960s, the field of German-American Studies in the Americas has rapidly expanded. There are now yearbooks for German-American Studies, German-Canadian Studies, German-Brazilian Studies, etc. It is in this period when the field gained acceptance as an academic field of study and research. Numerous centers, institutes, library collections, and other scholarly organizations were established and flourish today. The ethnic revival at the grass roots level, therefore, directly impacted on German-American Studies at the academic level. This, in turn, impacted on the local and regional levels where communities have displayed a great deal of interest and concern with their history and heritage. This dynamic interrelationship between the community and the academy is an essential element in the continued growth and development of the field.

Along with the recent rapid expansion of the field has come a veritable avalanche of publications, which clearly demonstrates the numerous possibilities for research in this area. A priority agenda item is the introduction of courses into the curricula at all educational levels which deal with the history, literature and culture of the German element. We now have the necessary foundations in place for this with numerous academicians now being involved and with numerous publicatiosn, scholarly organizations, and conferences. What is now necessary is the introduction of courses and programs dealing with German-American Studies, and the promotion of undergraduate and graduate research and study in cooperation with the many German communities. This needs to remain a primary concern and focus at least for the rest of the century, so that the field becomes firmly established in the curricula.

What, then, should be the role and responsibility and relationship of the various sub-branches in the field to one another? How should they relate to one another? As already stated, the primary focus for each sub-branch must be on the German element in its particular area, with building on the ethnic revival of the last two decades, and with the introduction of the field into the curricula at all levels. The foundation is there and it must be built upon.

If we ask questions regarding the nature of the relations of the various branches of the field, it is well to inquire as to the current status of such relations. First of all, there is, at present, a great deal of communication and cooperation in North America. For example, specialists in the U.S. belong to the German-Canadian Historical Association and attend German-Canadian meetings. A recent anthology of German-American Literature was compiled by a German-Canadian scholar. Second, the cooperation is geographically determined, which is to say that scholars in North America are working together, as are those in the South, but there is not a great deal of communication and cooperation between the two.

Although the primary focus should be on the immediate, one's own branch of the field, a secondary priority should be on the whole field of German-American Studies in the Americas. Placing this as secondary is appropriate, but it must at the same time be a priority, since at a future stage in the development of the field, there will be increasing communication and cooperation between scholars in North and South America.

Therefore, the present close interrelationships between German-Canadian and German-American scholars and organizations needs to continue. Second, the attempt should be made to establish this same kind of working relationship with South American scholars. This may take the following forms: small group meetings, conferences, seminars, lecture series, and exchange programs. The long-term future development of the various branches of German-American Studies requires this kind of communication and cooperation, just as scholars from other fields work and exchange information together.

On the basis of the strong growth and development of the field of German-American Studies, especially in North America in the last two decades, the 1990s should be the decade which will result in the integration of the field into the educational curricula at all levels. Although this will become a central focus, let us not lose sight of the fact that each branch is part and parcel of a larger field which spans the hemisphere, and let us do all that we can to further all avenues of communication and cooperation for the benefit of the German heritage, and especially for the benefit of the field of German-American Studies. (13)

Notes:

1. Paul Baginsky, *German Works Relating to America 1493-1800: A List Compiled from the Collections of the New York Public Library*, (New York: New York Public Library, 1942).

2. Regarding Rattermann, see Don Heinrich Tolzmann, *German-American Literature*, (Metuchen, New Jersey: Scarecrow Pr., 1977), pp. 240-44.

3. Regarding the work of Arndt, see Gerhard K. Friesen, *The German Contribution to the Building of the Americas: Studies in Honor of Karl J. R. Arndt*, (Hanover, New Hampshire: Clark University Pr., 1977). For a review of the work of Froeschle, see Don Heinrich Tolzmann, "Recent German-Canadiana," *Journal of German-American Studies*, 15:3-4(1980): 95-97.

4. Albert B. Faust, *The German Element in the United States*, (New York: Steuben Society, 1927).

5. Victor Wolfgang von Hagen, *The Germanic People in America*, (Norman: University of Oklahoma Pr., 1976), p. 7.

6. Excellent chronologies of the basic dates of German-Canadian and South American German history can be found in Hartmut Froeschle, *Die Deutschen in Lateinamerika: Schicksal und Leistung*, (Tuebingen: Horst Erdmann Verlag, 1979), pp. 848-70, as well as in his "Die deutsche Einwanderung und Siedlung in Kanada: Zeittafel und Bibliographie," in: Juergen Schneider, *Wirtschaftskraefte und Wirtschaftswege V: Festschrift fuer Hermann Kellenbenz*, (Stuttgart: Klett-Cotta, 1981), pp. 825-44. For the basic facts of German-American history, See LaVern J. Rippley, *The German-Americans*, (Boston: Twayne, 1976).

7. For an annotated discussion of works which deal with this period, see Don Heinrich Tolzmann, *Catalog of the German-Americana Collection, University of Cincinnati*, (Munich: K.G. Saur, 1990).

8. Regarding these events, see Gerhard K. Friesen, "The Presentation of German-Canadian Concerns in the Berliner Journal, 1914-1917," *German-Canadian Studies*, 6(1987): 138-52; Frederick Luebke, "The German Ethnic Group in Brazil: The Ordeal of World War I," *Yearbook of German-American Studies*, 18(1983): 255-67; and John Dunphy, "The Lynching of Robert Prager," *Illinois History*, 23:3(1984): 35-37.

9. For further information about the ethnic revival, see Michael Novak, *The Rise of the Unmeltable Ethnics*, (New York: Macmillan, 1971).

10. See Stanley Haidasz, "Multicultualism - A Tangible Reality," *German-Canadian Yearbook*, 1(1973): 11.

11. For a discussion of the church history period, see Don Heinrich Tolzmann, "German-American Studies: History and Development," *Monatshefte*, 80:3 (1988): 278-88.

12. Ibid.

13. With regard to future developments in the field, see the editor's forthcoming work *The First Germans in America, With a Biographical Directory and Index* which calls for the celebration in 2008 of the 400th anniversary of the arrival of the first German settlers in America at Jamestown, Virginia.

# PART TWO - SACHSE'S HISTORY

## Historical Introduction

WRITERS of American history have thus far failed to accord to the German people anything like the proper amount of credit due them for the part they took in making possible the voyages to the unknown lands in the west, which resulted in the discovery of this Continent. Nor do they chronicle what prominent factors the Germans were, from the earliest days of Columbus down to the present time, in the exploration, settlement and development of America, a name which, by the way, is of German origin; it originated with a German student and was suggested by him, and appeared for the first time in history upon a German map and globe.

Instances are extremely rare where the average historian has accorded any credit to the German people in connection with the history of this country. This applies with equal force to both northern and southern divisions of the western hemisphere. All matters relating to American history, which might redound to their glory, seem for some reason to have been hitherto studiously eliminated or cast aside by historians of all races, Latin, Celtic, British, and I may even say American.

It has been repeatedly stated that Germany, of all the chief nations of Europe, was the only one which took no active part or interest in the discovery or early settlement of the western world. This and other statements of similar import, so oft repeated, have become accepted as truth; and as a consequence, neither Germany nor her sons appear in the histories of the day as factors in America's early history. Yet notwithstanding this firmly rooted notion, as a matter of history it was due to the great influence exercised by Germany and the Germans over the trade of the world, during this transitional period, more than to any other circumstance, that eventually led, not only to the discovery of the western continent, but also to that of an ocean passage to India.

The injustice of these many biased statements has long been felt by such historical students and investigators at home and abroad as boast of either German birth or ancestry. The first person to give any practical expression to his convictions in this country, and thus revive an interest in the subject, was a Pennsylvania-German, or, more properly speaking, a German who had made Pennsylvania his home. It was Doctor Johann Matthew Otto,[1] one of the Moravian Brethren at Bethlehem, a well known scientist and medical practitioner of a century ago, and a

---

[1] Doctor Johann Matthew Otto, one of the Moravian Brethren at Bethlehem, one of two brothers both of whom were doctors, was a surgeon of note, whose reputation extended far beyond the bounds of the Brethren's community in Pennsylvania. Dr. Otto was born at Meiningen, November 9, 1714, and studied medicine first under his father, and then at Augsburg. He entered into his father's practice about 1740, but two years later came to America with a company of about sixty persons on the "snow" Irene. The party came via Holland and England, and reached Bethlehem on July 8, 1750. Dr. Otto at once became known as a surgeon of skill, and his services were called into requisition by the authorities during the French and Indian war, which swept over the Province. His treatment of the Indian Tatamy, as well as his reports to Governor Denny, are matters of record. He was elected a member of the American Philosophical Society, April 21, 1769. This was the first meeting held by the present Society after the union with the American Society, held at Philadelphia, for promoting useful knowledge. Dr. Otto was stricken with paralysis, August 7, 1786, and died at Bethlehem two days later. The following notice appears in connection with his burial upon the Moravian record: "He served the congregation and surrounding neighbourhood for thirty-six years with great faithfulness, by the Lord's help performed many difficult cures, and was held in high regard." (See Transactions of the Moravian Historical Society, vol. iv. part 2, pp. 62-64; also Memorials of the Moravian Church, vol. i.)

member of the American Philosophical Society, who addressed a "Memoir on the Discovery of America" to the Society in 1786 through its President, Dr. Benjamin Franklin, in which he boldly set forth the claims of Martin Behaim of Nürnberg, as a partaker in the discovery of America.[2] This paper was published in the "Transactions" of the Society,[3] and attracted great attention at home and abroad. It resulted in other investigators of greater and lesser degree taking up the study.

SEAL OF THE AMERICAN PHILOSOPHICAL SOCIETY.

Prominent among scholars who have given their attention to the subject are to be found the names of Baron Alexander von Humboldt, Doctor F. W. Ghillany, City librarian of Nürnberg, Doctor Sophus Ruge, of Dresden, Doctor D. Th. Schott, of Stuttgart, the exhaustive "*Fest Schrift*" of the city of Hamburg, two volumes quarto, published in commemoration of the discovery of America by L. Friederichsen, (Ham-

---

[2] In this paper Dr. Otto closely followed the argument of Wagenseil, Altdorf, 1682. (*Wagenseilii Sacra parentalia B. Georgio Frid. Behaimo dicata*, p.16 etc.) See also Humboldt, *Kritische Untersuchungen*, vol. i, pp. 220-224; and *Stuvenio Jo: Friderico, De Vero Novi Orbis Inventori, Dissertatio Historico-critica. Francofurti ad Moenum, Apud Dominicam a Sande Anno*, mdccxiv, 8vo. (Copy in Carter Brown Library.)

[3] Transactions, American Philosophical Society vol. ii, 1786, pp. 263-284. Memoir on the Discovery of America. (Reprinted London 1787. 4to.) A refutation of Dr. Otto's Memoir appeared in the *Memorial literario* (*Madrid*, 1788, *en la Imprenta Real, Jul. p.* 1784.) See V. Murr. p. 65.

## New History of Pennsylvania.   37

burg, 1892) and finally Dr. Konrad Kretschmer's monumental work, with its grand atlas of fac-simile plates, which forms a fitting tribute from the German Empire of to-day to the quadri-centennial of Columbus's initial voyage.[4]

What has been said with reference to the history of America in general applies with equal force to that of our own Commonwealth, the greatest upon the western hemisphere from an industrial point of view, and which, of all the numerous political divisions came the nearest to being a German one.

To clear up this lamentable state of ignorance and perverted history, at least so far as our own Commonwealth of Pennsylvania is concerned, the Pennsylvania-German Society, which is composed of men born in Pennsylvania of German descent, has decreed the compilation of a new and critical history of the Commonwealth. Each division or section is to be contributed by a member who has made some particular epoch in our history a special subject for study. In the carrying out of this laudable project, the writer has been requested to contribute a paper, which is to form the introductory

INSIGNIA OF THE PENNSYLVANIA-GERMAN SOCIETY.

---

[4] Festschrift der Gesellschaft für Erdkunde zu Berlin zur 400 Jährigen Feir der Endeckung Americas.

chapter of the new work. The theme given him is: "The Fatherland," showing the part it bore in the discovery, exploration and development of the Western Continent.

Now to comply with this task, I propose to go back to the pre-Columbian period, and in a concise manner to trace the political, social, commercial and religious changes from the time the Turk first obtained a foothold on European soil down to the period when Benjamin Furly, as William Penn's trusted agent at Rotterdam, turned the stream of German emigration Pennsylvania-wards,[5] a movement which resulted in the settlement of so large a portion of this fair province by our ancestry, where the various races united, settled, intermarried, and brought forth that sturdy race known all over this country for their industry, intelligence and thrift,—the "Pennsylvania-Germans."

I will also show you, in the course of my essay, how it was that nautical instruments, the result of German ingenuity, made it possible for the Genoese sailor to launch out beyond the sight of shore and traverse the wide ocean and the Sargasso sea, until he dropped anchor beside land which he imagined to be an outlying part of Asia.

Then as to the early settlement of the country, if the proper records could be found, they would show without a doubt that a number of the early naviga-

---

[5] See Penna. Mag. of History and Biography, vol. xix, pp. 277-305; also German Pietists of Pennsylvania, pp. 433 et seq.

tors were Germans[6] whose identity is now concealed under a Latinized or Hispanicized name, and that German industry and enterprise were well represented in both sections of the hemisphere.

As an illustration at this point I will merely touch upon two incidents:

Firstly, to tell you that, the first printer to embark for the new world was a German, who left Europe in 1534, his destination being an established German colony in America. This was fully six years prior to the venture of Jakob Cromberger, (Corumberger) also a German, to whom is usually accorded the honor of having introduced the art of printing into the western world. The oldest known specimen from the Cromberger press, a *"Manual de Adultos,"* bears the imprint 1540, *"en la gran ciudad de Mexico. . . . En Casa de Juam Cromberger,"* a fac-simile of which is here reproduced.

His second work, "An account of the great Earthquake in Guatemala," bears the legend *"Impresa en casa de Juam Cromberger, 1541."*

Secondly, let me ask how many students of American lore are aware that in the earliest days of our history, for a term of twenty years and over, one of the choicest portions of Spain's continental possessions in America was controlled, governed, settled,

---

[6] Several German Jews are known to have been with Columbus, on his first voyage. They were taken as interpreters, and in addition to the European tongues were versed in Hebrew, Chaldaic and Arabic. See Weltanschaung des Columbus, (Dresden 1876,) p. 21; also Die Endeckung Amerikas (Munich, 1859,) p. 79.

⸿Hristophorus Cabrera Burgensis
ad lectorem sacri baptismi mini
strū: Dicolon Icastichon.

Si paucis pnosse cupis: uenerāde sacerdos:
Ut baptizari quilibet Indus habet:
Qu" q̄ p⁹ ō bēt ceu parua elemēta doceri:
Quicqd adultus iners scire tenetur ité:
Quaeq̄ sient pscis prib⁹ sancita: porbem
Ut foret ad ritū tinet⁹ adultus aqua:
Ut ne ōspiciat (fors) tā sublime Charisma
Indulus ignarus terq̄ quaterq̄ miser:
Hūc māib⁹ vsa: tere: plege: dilige librum:
Wilinin⁹ obscurū: nil magis est nitidum.
Simplicis docteq̄ ōdit modo Uasc⁹ acut⁹
Addo Quiroga me⁹ psula bunde pius.

⸿Imprimiose este Manual de Adultos en la grā ciudad d̄
Mexico por mādado d̄ los Reuerēdissimos Señores Obis
pos d̄ la nueua España y a sus expēsas: en casa d̄ Juā Cromberger. Año d̄l nacimiēto d̄ nuestro señor Jesu Christo d̄ mill
y quiniētos y quarēta. A .xiiij. dias d̄l mes d̄ Deziēbre.

FAC-SIMILE OF THE EARLIEST AMERICAN IMPRINT KNOWN.

explored and developed by Germans and under German supervision. Yet such is an historical fact, as I shall proceed to prove, not only to your satisfaction, but also, I trust to that of other critics.

ARMS OF THE STATE OF PENNSYLVANIA.

## AT THE CLOSE OF THE MEDIEVAL ERA.

ARMS OF THE HOLY ROMAN EMPIRE.

A SURVEY of the political situation of continental Europe at the middle of the XVth century, presents a condition of comparative peace. Frederick III of the Austrian dynasty of Hapsburg, and the last emperor who was crowned at Rome, was on the Imperial throne of Germany; Constantine II was upon the Imperial throne of the eastern Empire at Constantinople. Thomas di Sarzano (Parentucelli) as Nicolas VI, occupied the Papal Chair at Rome. Charles VII was the acknowledged ruler of France; Henry VI was king of England. The first Christian held sway over Denmark, Norway and Oldenburg; Casimir III was king of Poland;

## Social Conditions of Germany. 43

James II ruled Scotland; and in the far East, Mohammed II succeeded Amurat as Sultan of the Turks.

As to the social conditions of Germany during this period, the chief aims of the German nation at large were the extension of their commerce, a revival of learning,[6a] and a release from narrow bonds, both religious and political. Two great factors appear opportunely at this time, to aid them in their efforts toward the coveted ends viz,:—the invention of printing,[7] and the improvements in making paper.[8]

It was in the year 1455 that Gutenberg completed his first great work. The effect of this invention was

---

[6a] It was about this time that the first mention of private schools appears in German History. These schools were separate and distinct from the various *Kloster-Schulen* and were established by the laity, who engaged teachers, not in monastic orders. *Vide Beiträge zur Geschichte des Schulwesens. Von Julius Hans. Zeit Schrift des Historischen Vereins fur Schwaben und Newburg*, vol. ii, p. 101, etc.

[7] The invention of printing, as we now use the term, dates from the discovery and use of movable wooden and metal types by the Germans Gutenberg, Faust and Schöffer (1440-1460) during which years the Bible was printed by them and the process of casting type was perfected. For earlier attempts at printing, see Knight's Mechanical Dictionary, pp. 1789, etc. Article Printing. The Chinese invented printing some 900 years before the Germans, and their art was described in Persian books. Had these books reached Europe earlier than they did, we should have learnt to print from the Chinese, instead of having to invent it for ourselves.

[8] The improvement in the making of paper here alluded to consisted in the use of linen rags for the purpose, and a method for pulping the fiber by beating. The first paper-mill in Europe for making paper from linen rags was established at Nürnberg in Germany by Ulman Strother as early as 1390. This mill was operated by two rollers, which set in motion eighteen stampers, a method which continued in use for over four centuries.

a widespread one, and was not confined by the bounds of the Fatherland, but rapidly extended into adjoining countries, where in every case it was introduced by German craftsmen.

GUTENBERG PRESS.

Gutenberg's invention was more than a mere mechanical triumph. It caused a rent in the veil of ignorance, so great that it was forever torn asunder, and opened to the average man the field of learning and literature, as at the same time it sealed the downfall of monastic and scholastic exclusiveness forever.

How important a factor Germany was in the subsequent enlightening of the world, is shown by the fact that the earliest printing-presses in every country were manipulated by German craftsmen. Even the first English book, Caxton's *The Recuyell of the Histories of Troy*, was first printed upon a German press, by German printers and upon German soil.[9]

Various organizations or leagues of the larger communities or cities had sprung into existence from time to time, having for their object a betterment of the condition of the educated classes, and mutual protection against the oppression and exactions of the nobility. One of the noted examples of this movement was the establishment of that dreaded

---

[9] A folio printed at Cologne, in 1471, at the request of Margaret of York, the wife of Charles the duke of Burgundy.

THE "BEHAIM" HOUSE AT NÜRNBERG.
SHOWING MURAL PAINTINGS.
(FROM PHOTOGRAPH FURNISHED BY GERMANISCHES NATIONAL MUSEUM.)

secret Tribunal in Westphalia, known as the Vehmgericht,[10] before whose mandates even the most unscrupulous nobles were apt to quail.

The most powerful organization, however, a strictly commercial one, and the most widespread and firmly united one in the old world of which we have any record,—was the Hanseatic League,[11] which virtually dates back to the middle of the XIIIth century. This was a commercial alliance or union between certain cities of Germany for the extension of their trade and for its protection, not only against freebooters at sea, but against government exactions, demands of petty rulers, and the rapacity of the robber barons. Other objects of this celebrated league

---

[10] The *Vehm-gericht* (Femgericht or Fem-court) was a criminal court of Germany in the Middle Ages, which took the place of the regular administration of justice (then fallen into decay) especially in criminal cases. These courts originated and had their chief jurisdiction in Westphalia, and their proceedings were conducted with the utmost secrecy. This system of secret tribunals was most terrible to noble malefactors during the 14th and 15th centuries. The last general Vehmgericht was held at Zell, in the year 1568.

[11] The Hanseatic League dates from the middle of the 13th century. A confederacy was formed of the cities of Hamburg and Lübeck, to mutually defend each other against all violence, and particularly against the attacks of the nobles This confederacy was shortly joined by other German cities, until the League consisted of no less than eighty-five cities and communities. About the same time four great factories or depots were established in foreign countries: at London, in 1220; at Bruges, in 1252; at Novgorod, in 1272; and at Bergen, in 1278. Diets were held at stated intervals by the League, which exercised judicial power at home and a strict discipline over its connections abroad. The laws prescribed to the agents of the English fur companies in America, such as the Hudson Bay Company, were patterned after those of the Hanseatic factories. The last Diet of the Hansa was held at Lübeck in 1630, when the old confederation was dissolved.

were the prevention of piracy and shipwreck, the increase of agricultural products, a development of the fisheries, the mining industry and the manufactures of Germany;[12] in fact, everything calculated to increase the wealth and importance of the nation.

HANSEATIC ARMS.
(LONDON.)

One of the chief results of the wise policy pursued by the Hanseatic League was the fact that everywhere throughout the known world the German merchants and traders became famous for their probity and enterprise. The influence of the League extended to England, Sweden, Russia and the lesser countries; and by the perfection of its organization and co-operation with the Venetians, the merchants of Germany at the period under consideration may be said to have controlled the trade of Europe, if not of the world.[13]

It is true that the Venetians and Genoese had a monopoly of the Mediterranean and Oriental trade, and virtually controlled Constantinople, then still the capital of the tottering Byzantine empire, and, like Alexandria, one of the great centres for East Indian

---

[12] Robertson's India (London, 1791,) p. 120.
[13] *Ibid.*

"THE STEEL-YARD" WAREHOUSES OF THE GERMAN MERCHANTS IN LONDON, IN XVI CENTURY.

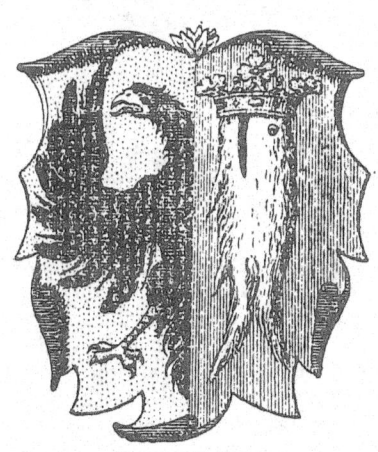

HANSEATIC ARMS.
(BERGEN, NORWAY.)

products. But it must not be overlooked that a continuance of their commercial prosperity depended almost entirely upon the German nation and Hanseatic League. It was from the mines in northern Germany whence came the gold and silver needed for their barter with

India,[14] while the Hansa distributed the goods thus obtained; first by land carriage, and again reshipping them from nothern ports. Then in return the Hansa supplied the Venetians and Genoese with the naval stores needed to build and maintain their fleet upon the Mediterranean.

Such was the condition of Continental Europe fifty years prior to the advent of the Columbian era;—comparative quiet reigned over the major part of the land; manufacturers and commerce flourished; wealth was accumulated by legitimate means; and the merchant and patrician, and not the feudal baron, were the mighty power throughout the land.

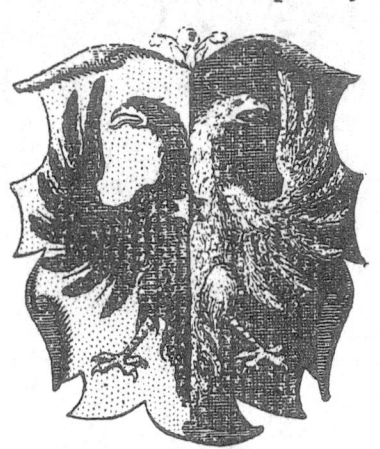

HANSEATIC ARMS.
(COMTOIR AT BRUGES.)

Scarcely, however, had the century passed into its latter half, when a disturbing element appeared on

---

[14] Robertson's India, p. 120. The gold and silver mines in the various provinces of Germany were the most valuable and productive of any known at that time in Europe. See Zimmermann's Political Survey of Europe, p. 102. The prosperity of these mines, mainly in the vicinity of Freiberg, continued until the influx of American silver from Mexico caused the price of silver to fall so low that the German mines ceased to be productive. This misfortune was hastened by the numerous wars, notably that known as the Thirty Years' War. See Festschrift zum 100 jährigen Jubilaeum der Königlichen Berg Academie zu Freiberg, 1866.

Mohammed II. (The Great).
Born, 1430. Died, 1481.

## The Capture of Constantinople. 49

the Bosphorus, which was destined to affect the whole political situation of Europe, and at the same time bring about the greatest changes in commercial circles,—an event which stimulated a series of voyages and eventually led to the discovery of the Western world.

This event was the capture of Constantinople, after a heroic defence under the German Germanicus[15] by the Sultan Mohammed II[16] in 1453, whereby the Turk not only obtained a foothold in Europe, but was at the same time in a position to control the most lucrative trade of the Mediterranean.[17]

The immediate effect of this Moslem occupation, so far as we are concerned, was two-fold: firstly, the expulsion, by the Turks, of the Grecian scholars who fled to Italy and Germany, and there obtained a foot-hold in the various universities of the two countries, bringing about, as we all know, the Renais-

---

[15] Johannes Germanicus (Johann der Deutsche,) a German soldier and scientist, who was the engineer in charge of the defences of Constantinople during this memorable siege. He successfully defended the sea approaches by aid of a monster chain, and by countermines foiled the Turks in their attempts to blow up the walls of the city. It was by the ingenuity of this brave German that the breaches made by day were successfully repaired by night, and for so many days the Cross defied the Crescent.

[16] Mahomet II, emperor of the Turks, succeeded his father Amurath in 1451. He was a warrior and religious fanatic. He had sworn to exterminate the Christian religion; and in attempting to carry out his oath he subdued two empires, twelve tributary kingdoms, and 200 towns, and was preparing to subjugate Italy when he died in 1481 after a reign of 31 years. His death caused a rejoicing throughout the whole Christian world.

[17] Robertson's India, p. 128.

sauce and the Reformation.  Secondly, the capture of Constantinople effected the expulsion of the Genoese from the Levant; a circumstance which while it proved the downfall of Genoa as a commercial centre, was yet destined to increase the influence, commerce and wealth of its rivals, the Venetians, who, by greater foresight or good fortune, had secured favorable treaties with the Sultan of Egypt, and became for the time being masters of the Mediterranean and of the commerce of the Indies.

ARMS OF GENOA, A. D. 1450.

The fortunes of the Venetians were so closely allied with those of the German merchants and Hansa, which united the north and south of Europe in commercial bonds[18] that German mercantile circles experienced an equal era of prosperity with their associates of Venice.[19]  Great fortunes were amassed by some of the German mercantile towns and their citizens.[20]  A notable instance was that of the city of Augsburg, the Augusta Vindelicorum of old, whose

---

[18] Robertson's India, p. 125.  Robertson says: "In some cities of Germany, particularly Augsburg, the great mart for Indian commodities in the interior parts of that extensive country, we meet with early examples of such large fortunes accumulated by mercantile industry as raised the proprietors of them to high rank and consideration in the Empire."

[19] *Ibid*, p. 125.

magnificent Town-hall with its golden ceiling,[21] is still shown to attest its former greatness and commercial glory.

The great fortunes amassed by the Venetians[22] naturally excited the envy and jealousy of other maritime nations, and the fabulous riches of the Indies formed the chief dream of the various rulers of countries bordering upon the seas. This feeling was heightened by the

ESCUTCHEON OF THE REPUBLIC OF VENICE.

---

[20] The most prominent among these merchants were the establishments of the "Welser-Geselschaft" and the firm of Raimund and Anton Fugger.

[21] The Golden Hall (*Golden Saal*) of the Rathhaus at Augsburg is still shown as one of the town sights. This hall, the second story of the Rathhaus, is a large room 32.65 metres long, 17.33 metres wide, and 14.22 metres high. It is lighted by no less than sixty windows. Its chief beauty consists in the fine panelled ceiling, richly carved and heavily gilded. It is also embellished with numerous symbolical and allegorical paintings. This ceiling is so called a flying ceiling, being suspended from the roof-timbers by heavy chains. Many fine paintings and relics are to be seen in the Saal and the four *Fürstenzimmer* adjoining.

[22] Towards the end of the fifteenth century, Venice was the richest and most honored community in Europe. It exercised a powerful influence in the commercial as well as in the political world; and it may be well said that her inhabitants comprised the most civilized people on earth,

HANSEATIC ARMS.
(NOVGOROD RUSSIA.)

glowing accounts of Cathay and the Island of Zipango related by Marco Polo,[23] fragmentary extracts of which appeared and were circulated in manuscript even before the art of printing was discovered.[23a]

One of the chief aims of all navigators was to find a way to reach by water, the El-Dorado described by Marco Polo. The great obstacle in the way, however, of maritime exploration was the lack of any method by which the navigator could tell where he was

---

among whom flourished all the arts and sciences. The wealth accumulated by some of her citizens was phenomenal, and was approached only by that of a few German merchants, who were in contact with both the Genoese and the Hansa.

[23] Marco Polo, the celebrated traveller, was the son of a Venetian merchant, who, with his brother, had penetrated to the court of Kublai, the great Khan of the Tartars. This prince sent them back as his ambassadors to the Pope. Shortly afterwards the two brothers, accompanied by two missionaries and the young Marco, returned to Tartary, and remained there for seventeen years, visiting China, Japan, several of the East Indian islands, Madagascar and the coast of Africa. The three Venetians returned to their native country in 1295, with immense wealth. Marco afterwards served in the wars against the Genoese, and being taken prisoner, remained many years in confinement, the tedium of which he beguiled by composing the history of the travels of his father and himself, under the title of *"Delle Maraviglie del Mondo da lui vedute, &c."* He ultimately regained his liberty; but of his subsequent history nothing is known.

Fra Mauro's
Weltkarte von 1459.
(Original in Venedig).
Längenmaßstab ¹⁄₁₀ des
Originals.

FRA MAURO'S MAP OF T:
SIZE ONE-TENTH
(FROM RUGE'S ZEITALTERS DER ENTDECKUNGEN.)

E WORLD, VENICE, 1459
OF ORIGINAL.

when out of sight of land. This problem was not solved until the German mathematician, Johannes Müller (Regiomontanus)[24] of Königsberg, calculated his Ephemerides,[25] and Martin Behaim of Nürnberg, perfected the astrolabe.[26] This brings us down to the last quarter of the XVth century. Portugal, under the wise reign of Henry, the Navigator, had gradually forged its way into the foremost rank of sea-faring nations, and was now

---

[23a] Marco Polo's Travels, a folio edition of this work was published in German at Nürnberg by Fritz Creusner as early as 1477. This was followed by another edition by Anton Sorg, at Augsburg, 1481.

[24] Regiomontanus, (Camillus Johannes Müller) b. at Königsberg, Franconia, in 1436. He studied at Leipsic, and then placed himself under Purbachius, professor of mathematics at Vienna. Later he became one of the most noted astronomers and mathematicians of his day. In 1471-1475 he sojourned at Nürnberg, where he built an observatory and established a printing-press, both under the patronage and by the aid of a wealthy patrician named Bernhard Walther, the local representative of the celebrated Welser firm of Augsburg. Here Regiomontanus printed the first German Almanac in 1474, calculated for the year 1476; the price for which was twelve golden gulden each. But five copies are known at the present day. His most important contribution to science was the publication of his astronomical observations, 1475-1506, under the title Ephemerides or Nautical Almanac. Notwithstanding the high price of twelve ducats per copy, the edition was soon exhausted. Among his many works, the most valuable are: *Calendarium ; De Reformatione Calendarii; Tabula magna prima Mobilis; De Cometæ Magnitudine Longitudineque; De Triangulis.* He also simplified the astrolabe and the meteroscope, and suggested various instruments for the use of navigators. Regiomontanus died in 1476 by poison administered by a jealous scientist.

[25] Ephemerides, in astronomy, a collection of tables showing the present state of the heavens for every day at noon; that is, the places wherein all the planets or heavenly orbs are found at that time.

[26] An instrument formerly used for taking the altitude of the sun or stars at sea. The instrument by that name used by the ancients was similar to the modern armillary sphere.

under the sway of King John II, an enlightened Prince who planned new expeditions of discovery to sail south along the western coast of Africa.[27] These ventures, in which the German merchants and the Hansa were well represented by men, vessels, and ship stores,[28] were conducted with ardor and scientific method.

To improve the study of navigation, King John established, prior to 1481, the celebrated *Junta de Mathematicos*, a board or commission of scientific men to examine the different nautical instruments, almanacs, calculations and maps of the period, and report upon their utility.

This commission consisted of Don Diego Ortiz, Bishop of Ceuta and Calcadilha,[29] together with

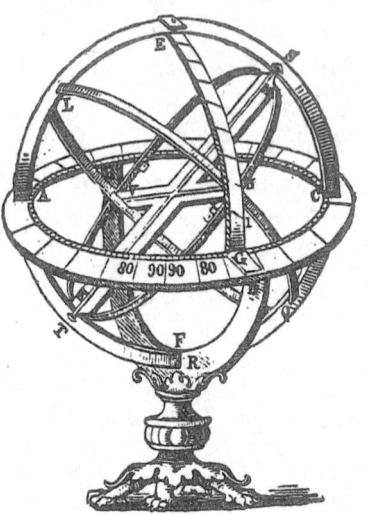

ASTROLABE OF THE ANCIENTS.

---

[27] The chief rulers of Europe at that period were: Friedrich III, Emperor of Germany; Alexander VI, Pope; Ferdinand and Isabella, Spain, Naples and Sicily; Charles VIII, France; Henry VII, England; Johannes Albertus, Poland; James IV, Scotland; Vladislaus, Hungary and Bohemia; Bajazet II, Sultan of Turkey; Johannes, Denmark and Norway.

[28] Kunstmann, Deutsche in Portugal. (München)—Ruge Endeckungsgeschichte der Neuen Welt, pp. 33-34. (Hamburg 1892.)

[29] Don Diego Ortiz was Bishop of Ceuta, but by contemporary writers

## The Junta de Mathematicos. 55

the king's two physicians in ordinary, Rodrigo [30] and Josef Judio (an Israelite) and the German cosmographer, Martin Behaim,[30a] a pupil of Regiomontanus, whose reputation as a mathematician and astronomer had preceded him. The three latter were

ROYAL ARMS OF PORTUGAL.

---

is usually called Doctor Calcadilha, as he was a native of Calcadilha in Galizia. It was he who, after Rodrigo and Josef had officially denounced Columbus's scheme as a *negocio fabuloso*, advised King John II, to secretly avail himself of the scheme disclosed by Columbus. Humboldt, vol. i, p. 232.

[30] Evidently Maestre Rodrigo Faleiro or Falero, an astronomer of note. Barrow Voyages, &c. London, 1818, p. 28.

[30a] Martin Behaim (Behain or Beheim, Martin von Böhmen, Martinus Bohemus, M. Boheimo, Martin de Bohemia), the celebrated German cosmographer, was a member of the ancient Bohemian family of Schwarzbach, and was born at Nürnberg, according to some writers in the year 1430, but more probably in 1436 (according to Navarrete, the same year in which Columbus was born.) According to Humboldt he was a descendant of Matthias Behaim, who in 1343 made the first MS. translation of the Bible into the German language (copy still preserved at Leipzig) and of Michael Baheim, one of the noted Meistersänger in 1421. Little is known of Behaim's youth. He appears to have been in the cloth trade, and in the interests of his house travelled to Venice in 1457. In 1477-'79 we find him in Mechelen, Antwerp and Vienna (Regiomontanus sojourned in Nürnberg, 1471-1475.) From 1480 to 1484, we find Behaim at Lisbon, where Columbus then was. In 1486 to 1490, he was at Fayal, and there married the daughter of Stadthalter Jobst von Hurter (Jobst Dutra) who was governor of the Flemish colony there. He returned to Nürnberg, 1491-1493, where he constructed his

constituted a sub-committee with the special injunction to discover some sure method of navigating the seas according to the altitude of the sun[31] and construct mathematical and nautical instruments suitable for the purpose.[32] It was upon this occasion that Behaim brought to the notice of the Portuguese the celebrated calculations and tables of his former tutor, Regiomontanus,[33] which had been printed at Nürnberg as early as 1474.[33a] He also here produced his improved astrolabe,[34] which was of metal, and could be attached in a vertical position to the main-mast of a vessel.[35] This was the first application of the

COMMERCIAL SEAL OF MARTIN BEHAIM

---

famous Globe. In 1494, he went to France, and thence to Fayal, where he appears to have remained until 1506. Returning to Lisbon, he died there, July 29, 1507.

[31] Dr. Sophus Ruge, Geschichte des Zeitalters der Endeckungen, (Berlin, 1881,) p. 98. Also Ghillany, Geschichte des Seefahrers Ritter, Martin Behaim, (Nürnberg 1853,) p. 53.

[32] Der verdienst Martin Baheim, (Dresden 1866,) p. 59.

[33] Von Murr, (Diplomatische Geschichte) questions the statement that Behaim was a scholar of either Regiomontanus or Bercalden, but is forced to acknowledge that he was well versed in mathematics and the science of navigation before he came to Lisbon, and that so far history is correct in stating that the fortunate discovery of application of the Astrolabe to navigation gave him the reputation of a leading cosmographer (v. Murr, pp. 68-69.)

[33a] The first edition of Regiomontanus's German Almanac was printed from wooden blocks. In later editions, printed in both German and Latin, and in his Ephemerides in 1475, moveable types were used. Gelcich, "Lösung der Behaim Frage" (Hamb. Festschrift, vol. i, p. 74.)

[34] Die Verdienste Martin Behaim, (Dresden, 1866,) p. 61.

[35] See Die wissenschaftliche Bedeutung des Regiomontanus (Dresden, 1866,) p. 63; also Humboldt, Ex. Critique, vol. i, pp. 234-5.

MARTIN BEHAIM.
(BORN 1429. DIED JULY 29, 1506.)

## The Astrolabe of Behaim. 57

portable astrolabe to navigation, and together with the Jacobstaff,[35a] also introduced by Behaim,[36] taught the sea-farer how to discover the position of a vessel at sea without the use of the magnetic needle, and long and intricate calculations. It was the introduction of these nautical instruments into Portugal,[37] together with the tables of Regiomontanus which gave the navigators of that land so

PORTABLE ASTROLABE OF MARTIN BEHAIM.

---

[35a] Gelcich, in his "Lösung der Behaim Frage," states:

"Es wird sich möglicherweise herausstellen, dass der deutsche Fachmann, wenn nicht durch Einführung des Jakobsstabes, so doch in anderer Weise, zu den schon angeführten noch wesentliche Dienste der Schiffahrt leistete." Hamburger Festschrift, vol. i.

[36] According to Fournier, (Hydryographie, ed. 1643) the Junto and more especially Behaim in the first instance, improved the nautical instruments of the period by the introduction of smaller portable astrolabes, and by furnishing mariners with tables of the sun's declination. Upon referring to any date these tables would furnish the requisite data, to obtain which it was formerly necessary to enter into long and difficult calculations.

[37] Shortly after the formation of the Junto de Mathematicos, Martin Behaim was commissioned to return to his native city of Nürnberg, and have the necessary nautical instruments made, and to obtain a number of copies of Regiomontanus's new Ephemerides. Upon his return to Portugal he was sent with Cao as cosmographer, to submit the new instruments to a practical test. (Ruge, Hamburg, 1892.)

great an advantage over their rivals.[38] Columbus, who was at that time a resident of Lisbon,[39] was well acquainted with the German Behaim and his mathematical research; and it is an unquestionable fact that the success of the Portuguese in discovering the Atlantic Islands, and of Behaim's voyage down the African coast,[40] sustained Columbus

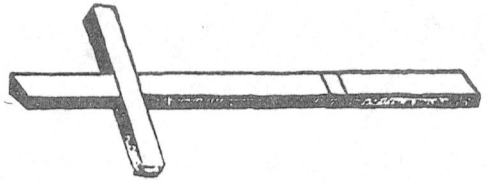

THE JACOBSTAFF.

in the hope of western discovery, if indeed it had not instigated him.[41]

Leaving out all claims that Martin Behaim had made any previous voyage to America,[42] and confining

---

[38] According to Humboldt (Examen Critique) the Astrolabe of Behaim was a simplification of or improvement of the meteoroscope of Regiomontanus.

[39] According to Dr. Ruge, Columbus first proposed his voyage of western discovery to King John of Portugal, about the year 1483, when his proposition was laid before the Commission de Mathematicos who reported adversely. The king, however, notwithstanding their report, was inclined to enter into the scheme of Columbus, had not the extraordinary demands made by the latter in the event of success precluded him from entering into negotiations so exacting with one who was a poor and unknown foreigner. (Zeitalter der Endeckung, pp. 231-2.)

[40] See Behaim's Entdeckungs-Reise an der Afrikanischen Küste mit Diogo Cao. (Ghillany, Geschichte, etc., pp. 41-51.)

[41] See Winsor, vol. ii, p. 35; Humboldt, Cosmos, English translation, vol. ii. p. 662.

[42] The claim of Martin Behaim rests upon a page in the Latin text of the Nürnberg Chronicle, which states that Cao and Behaim having

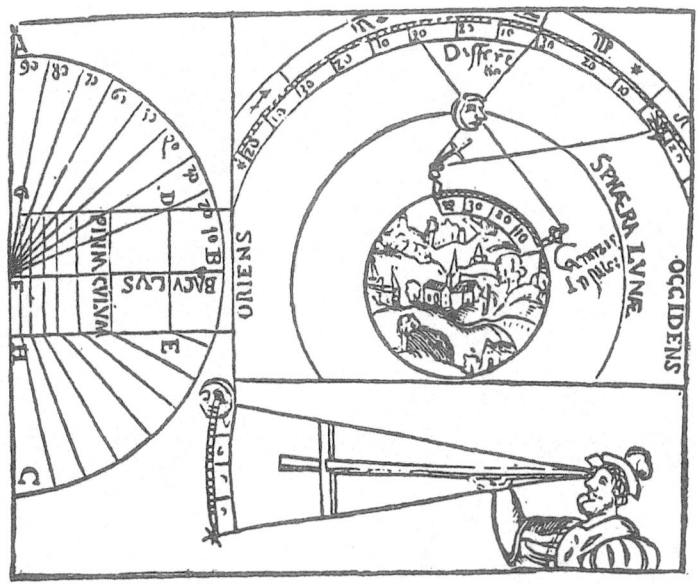

METHOD FOR USING THE JACOBSTAFF.
(From Cosmographia Petri Apiani et Genomae Frisii. Antwp. 1584.)

myself to incontrovertible facts alone, it will be seen that when finally the dream of Columbus was realized, under the patronage of Ferdinand and Isabella, it was made possible only by the aid of three great

---

passed the Equator, turned west and (by implication) found land, and thus discovered America. This claim, in the light of modern investigation, is not substantiated, as the passage referred to does not appear in the German edition of the same year; and on reference to the manuscript of the book (still preserved in Nürnberg) the passage is found to be an interpolation written in a different hand. It seems likely to have been a perversion or misinterpretation of the voyage of Diego Cao down the African coast in 1489, wherein he was accompanied by Behaim. That Behaim himself did not put the claim forward, at least in 1492, seems to be clear from the globe, which he made in that year, and which shows no indication of such a voyage.

.S.
.S. A. S.
X M Y
: Xpo. FERENS./

AUTOGRAPH AND SIGNATURE OF COLUMBUS FROM A LETTER DATED GRANADA, FEBRUARY 1502
"a los Reyes Catollcos exponiedo algunas observaciones sobre el arte de naveger.?"

## Sailing Craft of the Period. 61

factors, all of German origin:[43] The astrolabe of Behaim, the mariner's compass from the old German town of Nürnberg, and the Ephemerides of Joseph Müller.

SEA-GOING VESSEL, AT CLOSE OF XV CENTURY.

It is not known to a certainty whether there were any German adventurers in the original Columbus

---

[43] As a matter of fact, all the great navigators, Columbus, Gama, Magalhaens, owe their success to the improved German instruments of navigation. (Ruge, Berlin, 1881, p. 106.)

expedition or not.⁴⁴ Of the many private expeditions, however, which left Spain⁴⁵ and Portugal after the year 1495, the greater number were either projected or fitted out by the merchants of Germany or the Hanseatic League, and German adventurers bore no minor part.

It is a curious fact that both Columbus and Vespucci should die without knowing that they had discovered a new hemisphere;—both lived and died in the firm belief that they had but found the extreme eastern point of Asia.

---

⁴⁴ See foot note No. 6 *supra*.
⁴⁵ Winsor, vol. ii, p 132.

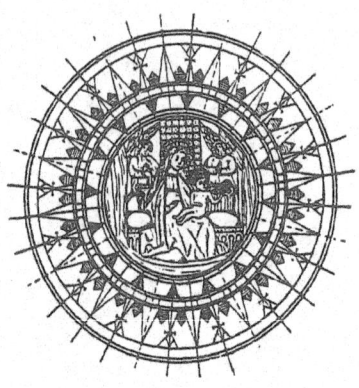

COMPASS "ROSE" ON DE LA COSA'S MAP,
A. D. 1500.

CHRISTOPHER COLUMBUS.
AFTER THE ORIGINAL PAINTING IN POSSESSION OF THE DUKE OF VERAGUAS.

## DAWN OF THE MODERN PERIOD.

ARMS OF COLUMBUS.

THE earliest published account of Columbus's initial voyage was a pamphlet containing the letter of Columbus sent, in March, 1493, to the royal treasurer, Raphael Sanchez.[47] It was almost immediately translated from Spanish into Latin by the learned Aliander de Cosco, and printed and circulated by the German printers, Frank Silber in Rome, and Ungut and Pohle, in Seville,[47a] by express permission of Pope Alexander. Four years later it was translated into German, and printed at Strasburg by Bartolemaus Küstler; the title and imprint are here reproduced in fac-simile. The curious woodcut upon the title shows the risen Christ appearing before the king of Spain and his suite. The Lord points to

Eyn schön hübsch lesen von etlichen inßlen
die do in kurtzen zyten funden synd durch dē
künig von hispania. vnd sagt võ großen wun
derlichen dingen die in dē selbē inßlen synd.

¶ Getüetschet vß der kantonischen zungen vnd vß dem latin
zü Ulm. Vnd ist etwas wz ein a steet dar zü gesetzet. auch dē
vnd es Ptolomeus vnd die anderen meister der casmographi
leren vnd schuben. wan der es funden hat der schuber es ee
vor dar von geschuben ist worden. vnd dem kunig ouch darvõ
gescit ist worden. Ee das er gesandt ist worden dz zü erfaren.

¶ Getruckt zü straßburg vff grüneck võ meister Bartlomeß
küstler ym iar. M.CCCC.xcvii. vff sant Jeronymus tag.

REDUCED FAC-SIMILE OF TITLE PAGE AND COLOPHON
Of the Earliest German Broadside Announcing the Discovery of America.
Original in the Royal Library at Munich.

¶ Epistola Christofori Colom: cui etas nostra multū debet: de Insulis Indiȩ supra Gangem nuper inuentis. Ad quas perquirendas octauo antea mense auspicijs τ ȩre inuictissimi Fernandi Hispaniarum Regis missus fuerat: ad Magnificum dnm Raphaelem Sanxis: eiusdem serenissimi Regis Tesaurariū missa: quam nobilis ac litteratus vir Aliander de Cosco ab Hispano ideomate in latinum conuertit: tertio kal's Maij. M.cccc.xciij. Pontificatus Alexandri Sexti Anno primo.

Quoniam suscepte prouintiȩ rem perfectam me cōsecutum fuisse gratum tibi fore scio: has constitui exarare: quȩ te vniuscuiusqȝ rei in hoc nostro itinere gestȩ inuentȩqȝ admoneant: Tricesimotertio die postqȝ Gadibus discessi in mare Indicū perueni: vbi plurimas insulas innumeris habitatas hominibus repperi: quarum omnium pro foelicissimo Rege nostro prȩconio celebrato τ vexillis extensis contradicente nemine possessionem accepi: primȩqȝ earum diui Saluato: is nomen inposui: euius fretus auxilio tam ad hanc: qȝ ad ceteras alias peruenimus. Eam vo Indi Guanabanin vocant. Aliarum etiā vnam quanqȝ nouo nomine nuncupaui. Quippe aliā insulam Sanctȩ Mariȩ Conceptionis. aliam Fernandinam. aliam Hysabellam. aliam Johanam. τ sic de reliquis appellari iussi. Quamprimum In eam insulam qua dudum Johanā vocari dixi appulimus: iuxta eius littus occidentem versus aliquantulum processi: tamqȝ eam magnā nullo reperto fine inueni: vt non insulam: sed continentem Chatai prouinciam esse crediderim: nulla tn̄ videns oppida municipiaue in maritimis sita confinib? prȩter aliquos vicos τ predia rustica: cum quorū incolis loqui nequibam. quare si mul ac nos videbant surripiebant fugam. Progrediebar vltra: existimans aliquā me vrbem villasue inuenturum. Denique videns qȝ longe admodum progressis nihil noui emergebat: τ hmōi via nos ad Septentrionem deferebat: qȝ ipse fugere exoptabā: terris etenim regnabat bruma: ad Austrumqȝ erat in voto cōtendere:

The first printed account of the discovery of America.
(Original Broadside in the British Museum.)

the wound in his hand; the king also points towards it in a manner to show that he comprehends the allusion. The explanation of the picture is that the king, in his dealings with Columbus, was long a doubting Thomas but now was convinced of a glorious realization. This account designates the Islands as "Isles of India beyond the Ganges."

The first printed account of the discoveries (dated edition) in which it was proposed to designate the new regions as a "New World" appeared in Augsburg in 1504,[48] "Mundus Novus.[48a]" In the following year, 1505, a German edition was issued at Nürnberg, "*Von der neu gefunde Region die wol ein welt genennt mag werden durch den christenlichen Kunig von Portugall wunderbarlich erfunden.*"

Thus far the new regions appear as "Terra Incognita," "Terra Nova," and later as "Terra Sanctae Crucis."

We now come to the naming of the western world —a question solved by Baron Alexander von Humboldt, while compiling his epoch-making work "*Examen critique de l' Histoire de la Geographie du Noveau Continent aux 15me et 16me Siecles.*"

---

[47] Reproduced in fac-simile.

[47a] Printing was introduced in Seville, Spain, in the year 1492, by two Germans Paul von Kölln, and Johann Pegnizer von Nürnberg, (Von Murr Deutsche Erfündungen, p. 727.)

[48] Augsburg, it will be remembered, was at that time an important centre of commercial activity, and its merchants were intimately engaged in the enterprises of both Spain and Portugal. Naturally the earliest and most authentic accounts would have reached that city.

[48a] Alberic Vespucci Laurenetio Petri Francisci de Medecis salutem plurima dicit "Mundus Novus."

("*Kritische Untersuchungen über die Historische Entwickelung der Geographischen Kenntnisse von der neuen Welt.* Ideler, Berlin, 1852.)

It was the above mentioned "Memoir on the Discovery of America," by Doctor Otto, of Pennsylvania, which gave Humboldt the incentive for this work;[49] and, strange to relate, this important feature of naming the New World is due to an obscure and unknown German geographer, Martin Waldseemüller,[50] (Hylacomus,) a young man from Freiburg in Breisgau,

---

[49] See Ghillany, p. 49; also Humboldt, Kritische Untersuchungen, vol. i, p. 224. He there states that Dr. Otto appears to have been entirely unacquainted with the Geography of the fifteenth century. See also footnote 2, *supra*.

[50] Martin Waltzeemüller (Waldseemüller) from Freiburg in Breisgau, was born about 1480-1481. He was a friend of the Alsatian Matthias Ringmann, a scholar of the celebrated philologus, Jacob Wimpfeling. In accord with the usage of the times, both men afterwards assumed Hellenized names: Waltzeemüller called himself Hylacomylus or Ilacomilus and Ringmann called himself Philesius, with the addition of Vogesigena, as his home was upon the Vosges. When, in the year 1507, a gymnasium and press were established at St. Die on the Meurthe, at the instance of the wealthy Canonicus Walther, under the patronage of the Duke Rene of Lorraine, both Ringmann and Waltzeemüller were called as tutors to the new College. Ringmann, while in Italy, became acquainted with the renowned mathematician and architect, Fra Giovanni del Giocondo, the friend of Vespucci, who translated the latter's letters into Latin, by which means the glorious results of the Florentine traveller became known to the two Germans, who also became admirers of Vespucci, and in 1507 had reprinted at Strasburg, Giocondo's Latin translation. When Waltzeemüller printed at St. Die his *Cosmographiae Introductio*, he incorporated the four letters of Vespucci. In connection with this work he conceived the plan of publishing a new edition of Ptolemy, the expense of which was borne by Walther Lud. This celebrated book did not appear until two years after the death of Ringmann, and was mainly the work of Waltzeemüller. It is in this edition that the celebrated map appears: *Orbis typus universalis iuxta hydrographorum traditionem.* This map was long supposed

Er hauptman der schiffung des mörs Cristoferus co-
lon von hispania schåbt dem künig von hispania võ
den inßlen des lands Jndie vff dem fluß gangen ge
nant. der do flüsset am mitten durch das lande in dia
in das indisch mör. Die er nelichen erfunden hat, vn̄
die zů finden geschickt ist mit hilff vn̄ groser schiffung. Und
ouch etlich vorsagung võ den inßlen. Des großmechtigisten
künigs Fernādo genant von hispania ¶ Nach dem vn̄d ich
gefaren bin von dem gestade des lands von hispania. Das man
nennet Colūnas hercules. oder von end der welt. bin ich gefaren in try vnd drysig tagen in das indisch mör. Do hab ich gefunden vil inßlen mit onzalber volcks wōhafftig. Die hab ich
all ingenōmen mit vff geworffnem baner vnsers mechtigisten
künigs. Und nyeman hat sich gewidert noch darwider gestelt
in keinerley weg. ¶ Die erst die ich gefunden hab, habe ich geheissen sant saluatoris. Das ist zů tuetsch des götlichen behal-
ters vn̄ selig machers. zů einer gedechtnyß syner wunderlicher
hohen maiestat die mir dar zů geholffen hat. vn̄ die von India
heissent sie gwanahyn ¶ Die ander hab ich geheissen vnß fro-
wen enpfengnyß ¶ Vn̄ die dryt hab ich geheissen fernandina
nach des künigs namen. Die vierde hab ich geheissen die hub-
sche insel. ¶ Die fünffte iohānam. vn̄ hab also einer peglich-
en yren namen gegeben. Und als bald ich kam in die inßel io-
hannam also genant do für ich an dem gestade hinuff gegen oc-
cident wertz, da fand ich die insel lang vn̄d kein ende dar an.
Das ich gedacht es wer ein gantz land. vn̄ wer die prouintz zů
Cathei genant. Do sah e ich ouch keine stert noch schlösser am
gestade des mörs, on etliche buren hÿser fürst vn̄d gestedel
vn̄ des selben glichen. Und mit den selben ynwonern mocht

a ij

---

Fac-simile page of broadside, containing the earliest German
account of Columbus' discovery.
(Original in the Royal Library at Munich).

who was then a tutor of geography in a school at Saint Die (Diey) in Lorraine, an out-of-the-way nook

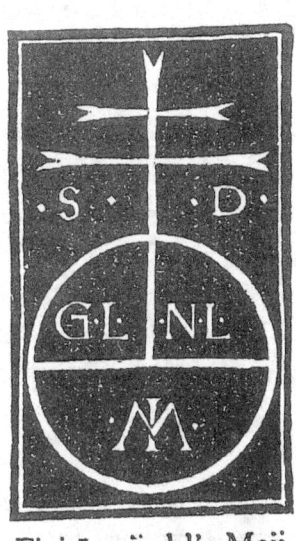

IMPRINT OF WALDSEEMÜLLER'S COSMOGRAPHIA INTRODUCTIO.

among the Vosges.[51] Here Waldseemüller[52] prepared a little cosmographical treatise, which was printed upon the college press, during the year 1507.[53]

---

to have been drawn by Vespucci. For a reproduction of it see Ruge, Zeitalter der Entdeckungen, p. 36; also Kretschmer's Atlas.

[51] Humboldt, Introduction to Ghillany, Geschichte des Martin Behaim, p. 11; Ruge, Zeitalter der Entdeckungen, p. 338.

[52] Humboldt, Kritische Untersuchungen, (Berlin 1852,) vol. ii, pp. 362, et seq.

Winsor, in his Critical History of America, states: "It was in this precious little quarto of 1507, whose complicated issues we have endeavored to trace, that, in the introductory portion, Waldseemüller, anonymously to the world, but doubtless with the privity

> Nūc v̄o & hę partes funt latius luftratæ/& alia quarta pars per Americū Vefputiū(vt in fequentī bus audietur )inuenta eft/quā non video cur quis iure veter ab Americo inuentore fagacis ingenij vi ro Amerigen quafi Americi terrā / fiue Americam *Ameri-* dicendā:cū & Europa & Afia a mulieribus fua for *ca* tita fint nomina. Eius fitū & gentis mores ex bis bi nis Americi nauigationibus quæ fequunt liquide intelligi datur.

FAC-SIMILE OF PASSAGE, WHERE THE NAME OF "AMERICA"
Is First Suggested, in the Cosmographiae Introductio of Hylacomylus of 1507.

of his fellow-collegians, proposed in two passages to stand sponsor for the new-named western world."

It is further an interesting fact that, in Spanish records, the official designation of the western hemisphere until the year 1550 was exclusively "Las Indies."[54] The name "America" does not appear to have been accepted by the Spanish authorities until

---

[53] *Cosmographiae Introdvctio | cvm qvibvs-dam | Geometriae | ac | astrono | miae principiis | ad eam rem necessariis | Insuper quator Ameici Ve- | spucij nauigationes. Vniversalis cdosmographiæ* [sic] *descripto | tam in solido quam plano, cis etiam | insertis quæ Pthol- omaeo | ignota a nuperis | reperta | sunt. etc.*

[54] Prof. Dr. Theodore Schott, Heft 308, Berlin, 1878, p. 28.

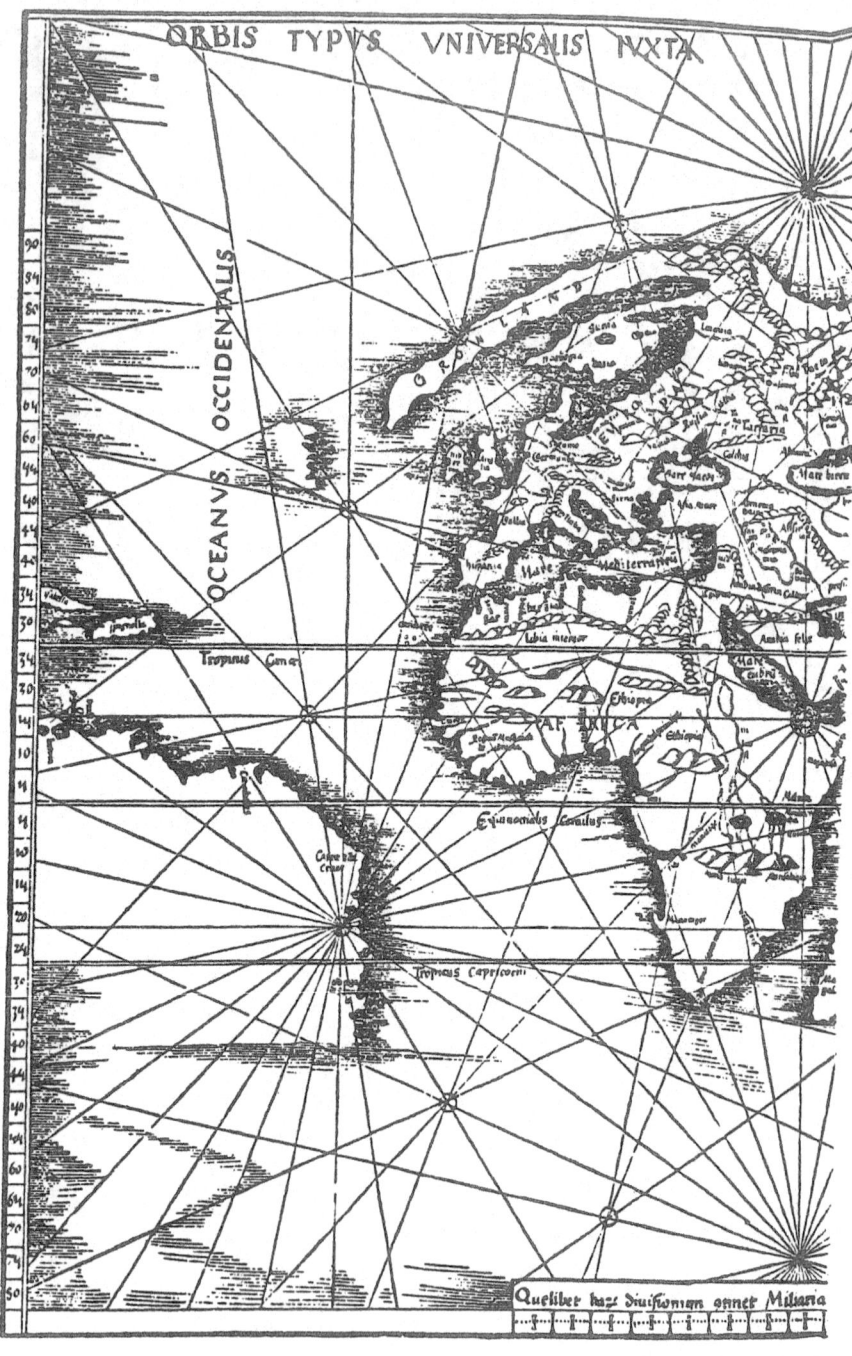

MAP OF THE WORLD, FROM THE STRASBU
(REDUCED FAC

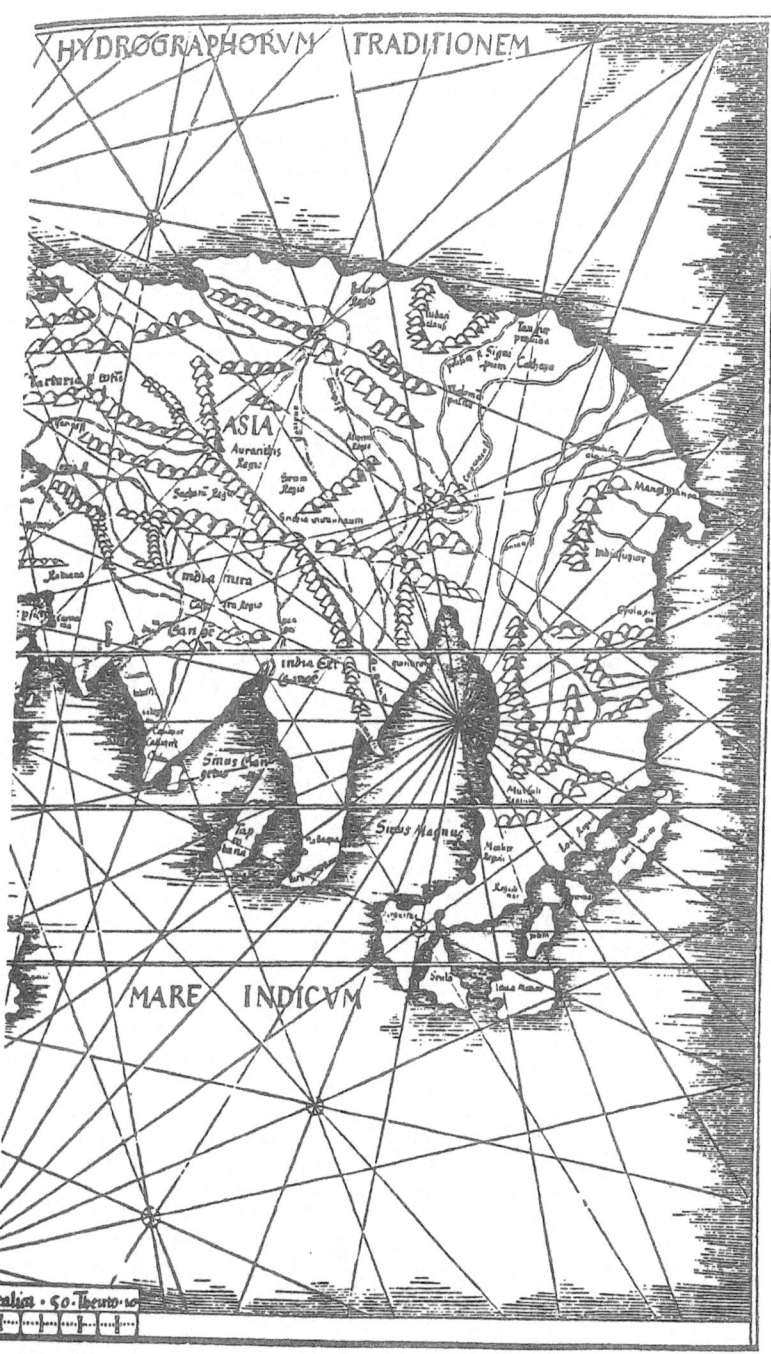

RG EDITION OF PTOLEMY, A.D. 1513.
SIMILE.)

the year 1758, when it appeared upon the Lopez map.⁵⁵

Thus was the new continent named. We now come to the derivation of the name "America,"⁵⁶ and we find that it is a strictly German one. Humboldt, an authority whom none will question, and who was further supported by the opinion of Professor Von der Hagen⁵⁷ of the University of Berlin, shows that the Italian name of Amerigo is derived from the German *Amalrich* or *Amelrich*, which under the various forms of Amalric, Amalrih, Amilrich, Amulrich, was spread through Europe by the Goths and other northern invaders.⁵⁸

In glancing over the cartography of the western hemisphere, it is also found that the first engraved map showing any portion of the western continent, before the name America came into use, was a German map engraved by Johann Ruysch as a supplement to the Latin edition of Ptolemy, 1508. The same was the case with the earliest map and the earliest terrestrial globe upon which the name

---

[55] It was not until the year 1600 that the two continents of the western hemisphere were officially designated as North and South America (*America septentrionalis* and *A. meridionalis*) by Jodocus Hondius. (Hamburger Festschrift ; Ruge, vol. i, p. 131.)

[56] The curious claim lately put forth by Jules Marcou, that Vespucci acquired his name Amerigo from some place in the western world, has been fully refuted by Prof. Ruge in Petermann's Mittheilungen, 1889, p. 121.

[57] America, ein ursprünglicher Deutscher Name.—Schreiben des Hrn. von der Hagen. (Neuen Jahr-buch der Berliner Gesellschalt für Deutsche Sprache. Heft, i, pp. 13-17.)

[58] Humboldt, Kritische Untersuchungen, vol. ii, p. 324.

America appeared. The former was the handiwork of another German, Peter Bienewitz, (*Petrus Apianus,*) a native of Saxony and one of the noted mathematicians of the day. In the same year, 1520, the German, Johannes Schöner, who for more than twenty years exercised a dominating influence in the cartography of the new world, as he kept pace with the new discoveries and issued globes with an explanatory text, completed the celebrated terrestrial globe which is still preserved in Nürnberg, and is distinctively known by his name. It is upon this globe that the name " America " appears for the first time.[59]

GLOBE OF PETER APIANUS.

It will thus be seen that the naming of the western continent, " America," was due entirely to the German geographers of the period, the example set by Waldseemüller, Apianus, and Schöner being eventually followed by the geographers and map-makers of all nations.[59a]

---

[59] See Catalogue Carter Brown Library, vol. ii.
[59a] See Kunstman, Altesten Karten Amerika's, p. 142.

## EFFECTS OF THE GREAT DISCOVERIES.

ROYAL ARMS OF SPAIN.

WITH the close of the medieval p e r i o d, a series of factors incident to the great maritime discoveries, appeared in rapid succession upon the political, social and religious horizon of Europe.

At the beginning of the present era, the discoveries made by Columbus brought little or no profit to Spain : as a matter of fact, none of the four voyages of Columbus even paid for the expense of fitting out the expedition.[60] The islands he had discovered proved to be in a primeval state, and required exploration, settlement and development. They were far different from what was expected from glowing descriptions of Zimpango and other islands in the far east as recorded by Marco Polo. In the islands visited by Columbus there were no signs of fabulous wealth, and but little or no gold,[61] silver or precious stones. A similar condition existed in regard to spices, silks and other Oriental fabrics. As a matter of history, in the earliest days of the modern period, Spain's western acquisitions were a greater source of expense to that kingdom than profit.

Far different, however, was the case with Portugal, then (1503) under the sway of an intelligent and liberal ruler, who welcomed and encouraged German learning and enterprise, and offered every inducement for German settlement within his domain.[62] Five years had hardly elapsed since Columbus returned from his first voyage, when Vasco da Gama, by the aid of Behaim's charts and Hanseatic vessels, sailed around the Cape of Good Hope, and thus found the long sought for way to India. This opened up at once a most lucrative commerce between Portugal

AUTOGRAPH OF VESPUCCI.

and the East Indies, in which German merchants and the Hansa were the chief factors. Special advantages were granted, every inducement was offered to these powerful organizations to aid them in developing the newly found route. An immediate result of this condition was that while wealth and commerce rolled in upon Portugal and the German merchants,[63] Spain was virtually impoverishing itself in the attempt to colonize and develop the new islands in the west.[64] The glory of Venice also departed with the loss of

MINIATURE.
(From Jean de la Cosa's Map of the Indies, A. D. 1500.)

---

[60] Columbus und seine Weltanschauung, Berlin, 1878, p. 23.

[61] Roderigo Bastidas of Seville, who visited the coast of South America from San Marta to the river of Darien in 1504, there found grains of gold in the sands This was the first time the metal had been sent in that state to Spain. (Bonnycastle, 161.)

[62] The first special grants by Portugal to German merchants and the Hanseatic League appear to be the Privelegium issued by King Alfonso V, March 28, 1452 (Document in full in J. P. Cassel's Privilegien und Freiheiten, welche die Könige von Portugal ehe den Deutschen Kaufleuten zu Lissabon ertheilt haben. Bremen 1771, 4to.) These special grants and concessions were renewed at different times by the reigning sovereigns of Portugal. Noteworthy among them are the grants issued by King Emanuel, January 13, 1503, conferring additional privileges

her monopoly of the Indian trade, which had formed the chief source of her power and opulence.[65] The great bulk of this trade was now diverted from the Mediterranean and taken around the Cape of Good Hope.[66] The German merchants were quick to adapt themselves to the new condition of affairs. At the very first sign of the decadence of Venice, when the tide of the East India trade turned towards Lisbon, we find Simon Seitz, an agent of the Welsers of Augsburg, installed in the capital of Portugal, and afterwards succeeded by one Lukas Rem,[67] who has left us a complete diary.

PRIVATE MARK.
(HANDEL'S MARKE.)
Bartalomeaus Welser and Company from letter August 18th, A. D. 1526, to Hans Ehinger, at Ulm.

---

upon the various merchants of Augsburg and other parts of Germany, who had established themselves at Lisbon at his invitation, or were there represented by resident agents or factors. (*Ibid*, p. 5; also Sartorius, Hanseatischen Bundes, Göttingen, 1808, p. 653.) The above was further extended under date of October 3, 1504. Upon March 16, 1508, King Emanuel confirmed two letters given to two German merchants releasing them from imprisonment unless condemned by a supreme judge. (*Ibid*, p. 10.) January 22, 1510, the right of citizenship was conferred upon all resident German merchants by King Emanuel. (*Ibid*, p. 15.) Numerous additional grants and privileges were issued and promulgated from 1511 to 1525 in favor of the German merchants and the Hanseatic League, such as releasing them from taxation, giving them the privilege of conducting transactions in excess of 10,000 ducats, etc. Perhaps the most curious concession granted the German merchants in Lisbon was the edict of December 23, 1524, which gave them the right to dress in their native costumes, and accorded permission for them to ride on horses or donkeys. (Cassel, Continuation, 1776, pp. 13-14; also Sartorius, p. 659.)

VENETIAN GALLEY (1486). From Breydenbach's Travels.

What was true of Portugal also applied to Spain; and as soon as definite accounts of the extent of Columbus's discovery reached Europe, we find the factories of the German merchants established at Seville. Long before the interdict against non-Spaniards was removed, the chief commercial establishment in the western world at San Domingo was in the hands of the Augsburg merchants, who had obtained special concessions from the king, and who had German vessels bringing cargoes back and forth.[68]

THE GRUBEL ARMS.

---

[63] The names of the leading merchants concerned in these enterprises were the Fugger, Welser, Hochstetter, Hyrssfogel and Imhof families of Augsburg and Ulm. As early as 1503 the Welsers had a resident factor at Lisbon, named Simon Seitz. A German expedition left Portugal for the East Indies, May 25, 1505. It consisted of three vessels, the San Raffael, San Jeronimo and Lionarda. Prominent factors in this venture were Balthasar Sprenger and Hans Mayr, both of whom left a diary and written account of the voyage. (Ruge, p. 148.)

[64] According to Las Casas, most persons who had up to that period (1518) settled in America were sailors and soldiers employed in the discovery and conquest of the country; the younger sons of noble families, allured by the prospect of acquiring sudden wealth; or desperate adventurers, whom their indigence or crimes had forced to abandon their native land.

Coincident with this commercial revolution, commenced the season of spiritual unrest in Germany, coupled with a desire to throw off the shackles of Latin bigotry and oppression, which resulted in the nailing of the ninety-five Theses against the church door at Wittenberg. The Reformation, which eventually overspread the whole of intellectual Germany, and which was followed by the efforts of Calvin and Zwingli, went far to break the power of monastic rule and priestly superstition, and was destined ultimately to prove an active agent in the settlement of Pennsylvania and the adjacent colonies by the yeomanry of Germany.

ARMS OF KELP V. STERNBERG.

Another important incident which falls within this

---

[65] Never did the Venetians believe the power of their country to be more firmly established, or rely with greater confidence on the continuance and increase of its opulence, than toward the close of the fifteenth century, when two events happened that proved fatal to both, viz., the discovery of America and the opening of a direct course to the East Indies by the way of the Cape of Good Hope. (Robertson, Ancient India, p. 130.)

[66] Ibid, America, Book, i, p. 79.

[67] Lucas Rem, (1481-1541) was a factor or agent of the Welser Company from 1499 to 1517, mainly at Lisbon. Later he became a partner in the firm of Endres, Rem & Company, and Chef of Endres & Lucas den Remen. His mother and daughter-in-law were both members of the Welser family.

[68] Welserzüge in America, p. 29.

MARTIN LUTHER.
BORN NOV. 10, 1483, DIED FEB. 18, 1546
FROM PAINTING BY LUCAS CRANACH IN THE PINAKOTHEK AT MUNICH

stipendia forent propter que sedes apostolica ascnescet plaueda. Et a censuris et penis a excomunicacionis° omnibus° q Jne-
re p̃ ut p̃ kriuea qucciꝰ. Diuulgatꝭ zlicoꝭ apostolice resiuatis semel dumtaxat Si non residuatis vero eisdem sedi to-
ciens quociens to peccatis ac semel in vita z in mortis articulo plenariam omniu̅ peccatoꝝ suoꝝ indulgenciā z re-
missione̅ impendere Ñon obstantibus quibuscunq̃ resiuacionibus a prefato pontifice vt eius preoecessoribus factis.
Dut in bulla data M CCCC LXXX. pridie nonas Decembris pōtificatus eiusdem anno decimo plenius ̃otinetur
Jn cuius rei fidem et testimonium. Ego frater Jobannes kaufman Ordinis minorum subcommissariꝰ eiusdem
sanctissimi domini nostri Summe pape, q̃ a ̃rre sup prefato negocio deputatus presence littere sicut sedi z sigilli tru
clare impressione munuit Anno domini M. CCCC, LXXXij. die

Forma absolucōis Misereatur tui omnipotens deus etcetera. Dominus noster ihesus xp̃s p̃ suam pissimam
̃am te absoluat z auctoritate eius a beatoꝝ Petri z pauli apostoloꝝ ac sanctissimi domini nostri pape
mihi ĩ hac parte ̃cessa. Ego te absoluo a vinculo excommunicacionis si incidisti z restituo te sacramentis ecclesie
et vniom et pticipacioni fidelium Et eadem auctoritate te absoluo ab omnibus tuis peccatis delictis z peccā
tis cum quacunq̃ grauibus et enormis. Etiam si talia forent ꝓpter que sedes apostolica silence esset ac de ipsis
eadem auctoritate tibi plenariam indulgenciā z remissionem. Dero. In nomine patris. et filij et spiritussancti Amen.

Jta q̃ in morte articulo adiungatur est hec clausula. Si ab illa ̃gritudine non decesserie, plenarias remissionem z indulgenciā tibi reservo auctoritate in morteis articulo secundu̅ccessurus.

FRAGMENT OF A PAPAL INDULGENCE, 1482, ORIGINAL IN POSSESSION OF THE WRITER.

period was the accession to the throne of Spain (1516) of Charles, the son of Philip, arch-duke of Austria and grandson of Ferdinand and Isabella. He, upon the death of Maximilian, was elected emperor of Germany,[69] thus for a time uniting the interests of Spain and the Fatherland.[70] The precarious condition of the finances of Spain, caused at the time by the drain of the unremunerative acquisitions in the west, induced Charles to look to the merchants of the powerful Hanseatic League for assistance. Among those applied to were the patrician families of Welser[71] and Fugger at

AUTOGRAPH OF EMPEROR CHARLES V.
(From Original in the Dreer Collection.)

---

[69] The rulers of Europe at this period were: Emperor, Charles V; Pope, Leo X; Spain, Charles I; France, Francis of Valois; England and Ireland, Henry VIII, (the first ruler to assume this dual title); Turkey, Soliman II; Poland, Sigismundus I; Scotland, James IV; Denmark and Norway, Christian II; Hungary, Ludovic II; Bohemia, Vladislaus; Sweden, Gustavus (Biorn), elected after the expulsion of the Danes.

[70] When the young king arrived in Spain from the Low Countries, he was accompanied by many of the Flemish and German nobility, who were in the confidence of the monarch, and were at once invested with almost every department of administration, among which was the direction of American affairs

[71] The Welser Company, at the time of our period, consisted of Anton Welser. Conrad Vöhlin and others. The chief houses were in Augsburg and *Memmingen*. Anton Welser's wife was Katharina Vöhlin (Vogelin, Fegelin) a daughter of Hans Vöhlin, a leading merchant of *Memmingen*,

## The German Bankers. 79

Augsburg.[72] Large loans were negotiated from both, and among the securities given were the choicest parts of Spain's possessions in America. The northern part of South America fell to the portion of the Welser family, and became known as Welserland, now Venezuela. The extreme southern and western part of the continent, almost immediately

---

and a sister to Konrad Vöhlin. In 1518, the firm came into possession of the Brothers Bartholomaeus and Anton Welser, sons of Anton Branch houses were then opened at Nürnberg and Ulm. Toward 1540, there were admitted to the firm Bartholomew's three sons: Bartholomaeus (2), Christoph. and Leonhard; his son-in-law, Christoph *Peutinger;* and Jacob Rembold, father-in-law of Welser's son Hans, together with the two Hans Vöhlin's son and nephew of his uncle Konrad. Of these latter Hans Vöhlin was the resident member of the factory at San Domingo (1534-1539) and upon his return. the elder Bartholomaeus, towards the close of the year 1540 sent his eldest son to America to take charge of the government of Welserland. In the year 1553 the elder Bartholomaeus retired from the firm, when the company was reconstructed under the name of Christoph Welser and Company. It was under this firm that the formal loss of Welserland and its reversion to the Spanish crown occurred in 1555 The great banking house failed in 1612. Bartholomaeus Welser. the elder, was the chief spirit in all the East Indian (1505) and American (1526-1555) ventures. It was also at his instance that the early broadsides giving the news of America were sent to Augsburg, and thence reprinted in German. A family history of the Welsers was compiled by the late Johann Michael Anton Freiherr von Welser (ob 1875,) but unfortunately is still in manuscript. See Anmerkungen zur Geschichte der Welserzuge. Hamb. 1892

[72] The old imperial city of Augsburg has thus far failed to receive in history the proper credit due to its former greatness and its position in the commercial world. The same is true of the German merchants: they have ever been deprived of the honor due them for their sagacity and enterprise in many brilliant epochs when they controlled a large portion of the trade of the world. This praise and credit is usually accorded to their rivals. (Arthur Kleinschmidt: *Augusburg und Nürnberg und ihre Handels Fürsten.* Kassel. 1881.)

after the discovery of the straits between the main land and Terra del Fuego, whereby the bounds of the hemisphere were defined, fell, for the time being, to the lot of the Fugger establishment.

Here again German learning and ingenuity had asserted itself, as it was by the aid of Martin Behaim's charts [72a] that Magellan was enabled to find and sail through the straits which now bear his name, and thus circumnavigate the world.[73]

---

[72a] In the early printed accounts, the Straits are frequently called *Fretum Martini Bohemi.* See *Cosmographia disciplina.* Basil 1561, 4to and Ludg. Bat. 1636 16mo Edit. tert, Cap. ii, p. 22. Also Diplomatische Geschichte. Gotha 1801, p. 82 *et seq.*

[73] *Die Verdienste Martin Behaim's* (Dresden, 1866, p. 61. See also Herrera and Pigafetta. Lösung der Behaim Frage; *Gelcich,* Hamburg 1892, p. 65 *et seq.*

## THE EARLIEST ATTEMPT AT GERMAN COLONIZATION.

ARMS OF CITY OF AUGSBURG.

FROM this period (1522) date the first systematic atttempts at German colonization in America, which, though interrupted for a time, were destined to be resumed as years passed by; and I venture to say, that if a census could be taken to-day of the population of the whole hemisphere, from Baffins Bay, to the Straits of Magellan, it would be found that German influence and commercial enterprise are predominant.

As the interesting facts connected with these early attempts at German colonization are not universally known, having been largely lost sight of by the Hispanicizing of German narratives and names, a few particulars of this important episode in America's history will not prove amiss.

It is well known to students of European history, that Charles V, who united so many crowns upon his head, and concentrated so much power in himself, was engaged by his ambition, or by the jealousy of his neighbors, in endless disputes, the expenses of which exceeded his resources.[74] In his dire necessity he was apt to turn to the patrician merchants of Augsburg and Ulm.[75] These appeals were not in vain, and ultimately his indebtedness to the two houses of Welser and Fugger alone amounted to over twelve tons' weight of gold.[76]

The Prince offered the former, as security for the vast loan, a large tract of land in America extending two hundred *Stunden*, (*Leguas*) along the coast,[77] which they accepted as a fief of Castile. From documents in the Indian archives at Seville,[77a] it appears that a special concession was

"A LANDS-KNECHT" OF THE PERIOD.

---

[74] Raynal's History of the Indies, vol. iv, p. 69.

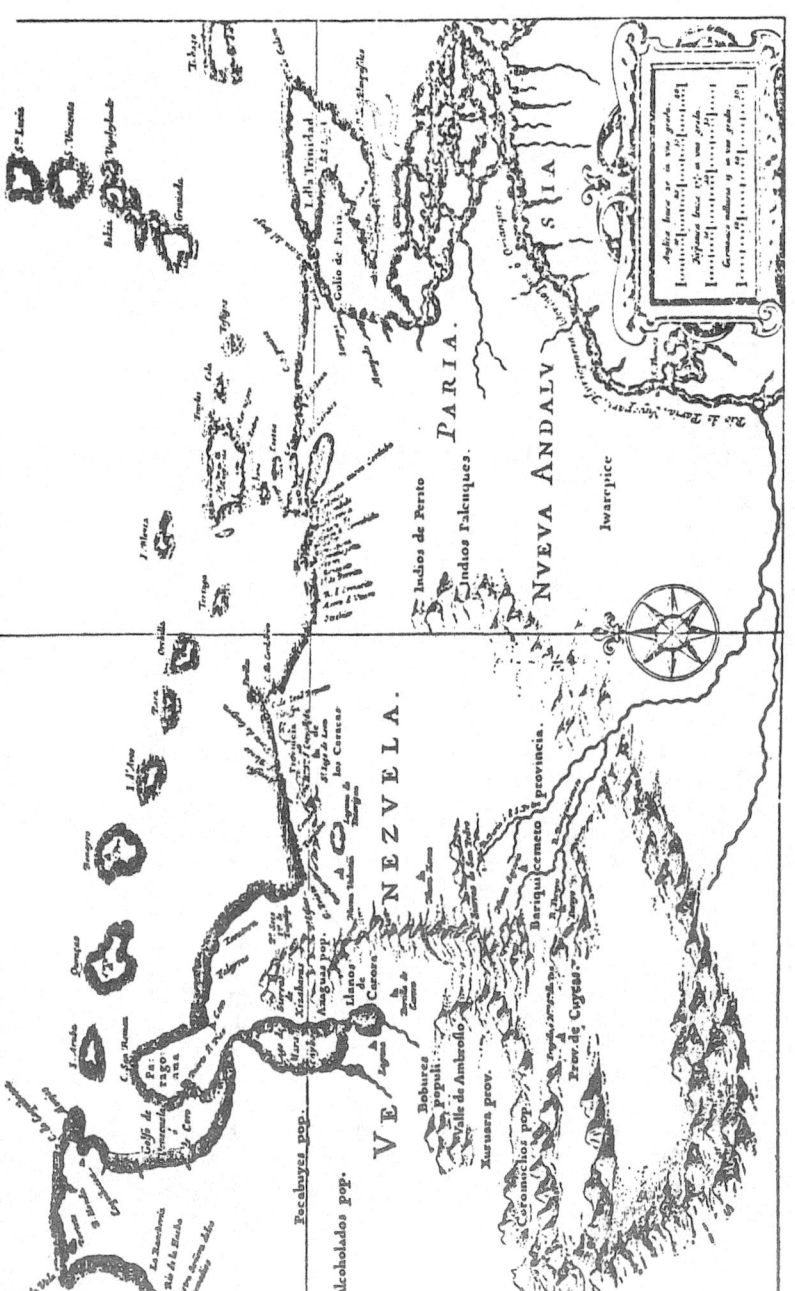

OLDEST KNOWN MAP OF "VENEZUELA" FROM DELAET'S NOVUS ORBIS, ETC., LUGUNDI 1633.

granted by the king to the Welser firm at an early date, with permission to establish a factory or trading station at San Domingo, a city which it was intended should be the metropolis of the new world. After the lapse of a year or two we find the Germans established there under Ambrose Dalfinger, (Ehinger)[78] and in control of the whole commerce

---

[75] An official list of patrician families of Augsburg engaged in mercantile pursuits at this period contains the following names: Adler, Arzt, Baumgärtner, Ehinger, Fugger, Herwart, Hochstatter, Ilsing, Imhof, Koch, Köler, Langmantel, Mänlich, Mayr, Neidhardt. Peutinger, Pfister, Pimel, Rehlinger. Rem, Rembold, Rentz, Sayller, Schellenberg, Seitz, Stetten, Vöhlin, Walther, and Welser.

[76] The indebtedness of the Emperor to the Welser Company is variously stated by contemporary accounts to have been from five and one-half to twelve tons of gold. See Weyermann, Nachrichten. (Ulm, 1829.)

[77] See *Novus Orbis* (Lunduni Bat, 1633); also Marci Velseri *Opera Historica. Provincia in America. Velseri patricii Augustani, etc.* (Chris. Arnoldus, Norimbergiae, 1772.)

[77a] The original documents relating to the Welser grants have lately been found in the British Museum at London. (Catalogued among the Spanish Mss. under the title: *Cedulas reales tocantes á la provincia de Venezuela 1529 a 1535*.) The volume is known as the "Welser Codex;" it consists of 159 folios of heavy paper upon which are engrossed 191 different acts, all relating to the Welser grants in South America. These documents extend from September 23, 1529, to May 11, 1535. Many of these papers are written in an almost undecipherable hand. The value of this MSS. will be appreciated when it is understood that all the various royal concessions to the firm of Welser and Company within the above period are recorded here. The volume is bound in parchment and the covers are secured with curious leather thongs. Just how this document was abstracted from the Indian Office at Seville, and found its resting place in the Manuscript room of the British Museum does not appear. This valuable find was thoroughly examined in 1894 by Doctor Konrad Haebler of Dresden, who published extracts and comments of the same in the Allgemeine Zeitung, München, Dec. 1894. See also "*Welser und Ehinger in Venezuela.* Haebler *Zeitschrift für Schwaben und Neuburg*, Augsburg 1894.

THE PENNSYLVANIA-GERMAN SOCIETY.

BARTHOLOMAEUS WELSER.
BORN 1484; DIED 1561.

FROM MEDAL IN CABINET OF THE GERMANISCHE NATIONAL
MUSEUM, NURNBERG, GERMANY.

and carrying trade of the new world. About the year 1526, Dalfinger, who, according to his instructions, had investigated the probable value of the Emperor's grant to his principals, returned to Europe, and advised his superiors to accept the security.

Patents were then issued by the crown, under date of March 27, 1528, granting the right of possession to Bartholomä and Anton Welser,[78b] their heirs and assigns, for the northern portion of South America, extending from *Cabo de la Veta* to *Cabo de Marcapana*, bounded by San Marta in the west, and Paria in the east.[79]

Heinrich Ehinger, of Ulm, merchant,[79a] knight of Santiago and royal chamberlain, together with Hieronymus Sailer,[80] were named as their agents.[80b] It is further stipulated by the king that the Welsers, through Heinrich Siger[81] and the

MARCUS VELSERUS.
Consil. Cæs. et Duumvir August.

---

[78] Ambrose Dalfinger [Talfinger] in Spanish documents, Micer Ambrosio, also Micer Ambrosio Alfinger. There appears to be more or less uncertainty as to the identity of Ambrose Dalfinger, some authorities in both Germany and Spain holding to the theory that Ambrose Dalfinger was in reality an Ehinger. This theory is partly based upon the Concession of March 27, 1528, which reads verbatim: "*Primera-*

above named Hieronymus Sailer[81a] their agents, should deliver, within a given period, not less than 4000 negro slaves to the royal colonies in the West Indies.[82]

In return it was agreed that all communication henceforth with this part of the Indies, whether from Europe or Africa, should be by vessels owned or controlled by the Augsburg firm of Welser and Company.[83] Arrangements were now made for the immediate possession, exploration, development, and settlement of the newly acquired territory, which was named Welserland.[84] The first expedition and German colony, consisting of about 500 persons,

ARMS OF THE EHINGER FAMILY.

---

*mente cumpliendo vos lo quo os ofreceis en ir o embiar la dicha armada con el dicho nuestro governador de Santa Marta é pacificando aquella como dicho es, vos doy licencia y facultad para que vos o qualquier de vos y en defecto de cualquier de vosotros Ambrosio é Jorge de Einguer, hermanos de vos el dicho Enrique, o qualquiera dellos, podais descubrir,* etc." The argument is further strengthened by the entry in the *Historia de la Conquista de Venezuela;* Oveido y Baños, Duro Edition vol i, chap. iv. *"Asistian por aquel tiempo en la corte de nuestro emperador Carlos V, Enrique de Alfinger y Jeronimo Sailler, agentes y factors de los Belzares,* etc." From the above it would certainly appear that if

## Departure from Europe.

who were all Germans [85] set out from San Lucar with that of Gracia de Lerma, who was interested in the adjoining colony, known as Santa Marta. The German contingent was under the command of Ambrose Dalfinger, the late factor at San Domingo, who now was commissioned as governor of the new colony, and Bartholomäus Sailer, his lieutenant.[86] The party consisted of soldiery, 400 foot and 80 mounted men, the latter under command of Casimir of Nürnberg;[86a] a number of German miners[86b] (*Bergknappen*); negro slaves; and a full band of

ARMS OF THE IMPERIAL CITY OF ULM.

---

Heinrich Ehinger was an Alfinger, his brother Ambrosio de Alfinger must also have been an Ehinger. See Dr. K. Haebler Zeitschrift der Gesellschaft für Erdkunde zu Berlin vol xxvii, p. 419.

[78b] Although the first royal concession made at Seville, March 27, 1528, as well as the amplification granted April 4, 1529, was apparently made to Sailer and the Ehinger brothers in fee-simple, the grant was in reality for the Welsers as stated in above text. Positive proof of the above is presented by a document in the Welser Codex in the British Museum; wherein Ehinger and Sailer as *repentant sinners* transfer all their right and title to their principals and further state, that, although the grant

musicians, playing chiefly of fifes, trombones, bass kettledrums, pauken and tambours. These men were enlisted and organized for the purpose of inspiring the natives.[87]

---

was secured in their names, they acted collectively and exclusively as agents for Bartholomaeus Welser and Company.

[79] The actual bounds of Welserland are not definitely known. Even Herrera, *Historia* ii p. 311, 1528, merely gives them in a general manner. The grant evidently covered a large tract extending rom the Province of San Marta well towards the Atlantic Ocean. The distance into the interior was evidently unlimited.

[79a] Heinrich Ehinger was evidently the trusted representative of the Welser company for many years, if he was not a full partner. We first meet with him in the present investigations at the Imperial Court at Saragossa, January 9, 1519, where he, together with Sebastian Schopperl, issues two drafts on Anton Welser and Company, in favor of the Emperor Charles V. Again at Saragossa he appears July 4, 1521, as a witness to the Testament of Simon Seitz. Later in 1522-3 we find him at Seville, where upon the arrival of Maghelhaes vessel "Victory" from the first circumnavigation of the Globe, he purchases for the German merchants the entire cargo of Spices brought from the East Indies. Five years later he appears, together with Hieronymus Sailer in the Venezuela contract.

[80] Haebler, Koloniale Unternehmungen im xvi Jahrhundert. (Berlin 1892.) p. 406.

[80b] For a full insight into this phase of the royal grant, see Dr. Haebler's comments upon the Welser-Codex. From this it would appear that the Ehinger Brothers together with Sailer attempted to hold the concession independent of the Welser Company. See foot note 78b.

[81] Ciguer in Herrera. Liguer in original.

[81a] As late as March one of these documents was to be found in the *Deposito historografico* of the Spanish government at Madrid. It bore the following title: "*Ano de 1526. Asiento y Capitulacione de los Alemanes Enrique Liguer y Geronimo Sailler, Obligandose a' hacer una Armada de 4 Narrios con 200, hombres o mas Armados y harrtuallados por imano, para la pacificacione y poblacion dela Provencia de Santa Marta.*" A transcription of this document was made in 1857 for the late Samuel Barlow, Esq, of New York. It consisted of thirty-four pages folio. At the public sale of that library, it was sold to an unknown purchaser for the sum of three dollars.

THE ARRIVAL OF THE WELSER EXPEDITION AT CORO, FEBRUARY 23, 1528. (Reduced fac-simile of a contemporary print.)

The fleet of four heavily laden vessels towards the end of 1527, arrived safely at San Domingo, where they reported to Sebastian Rentz,[88] Welser's factor,[89] and successor to Dalfinger.

After landing the Spaniards under de Lerma, the voyage was continued to the South American coast,

---

[82] From the above it would appear that the Welser Company were active agents in the development of the African slave trade. In this phase of our history, their commercial rivals, the Fuggers, stand out in glowing contrast. See above.

[83] According to Oviedo (Weyland, p 35) the Welser Company agreed; (1) To build within two years two cities and three forts within their possessions. (2) Four ships were to be sent out during the first year at their own cost, taking out at least 300 Spaniards and 50 Germans, who were to explore the various Spanish possessions in the Indies, and prospect for gold and silver mines; the Welser Company to have the right to work and develope all such mines. (3) The Emperor conferred the title of *"Adelantado,"* or Stadthalter, upon such persons appointed by the Welsers. (4) The Emperor granted to the Germans the right to enslave all such Indians as would not subject themselves to their authority except by force of arms. Oviedo goes on to state that only such portions of the above contract were complied with, as reverted to the profit of the Germans.

[84] Although "Welserland" for years was the accepted name for this Province (exclusively so in Germany), in official Spanish documents, so far as known to the writer, it was usually called Venezuela. Bonnycastle, who, in his history of Spanish America, closely follows Las Casas, gives the following explanation of the derivation of the name Venezuela. "The shores in the immediate vicinity of its waters (Lake Maracaybo) are unhealthy, owing to the vapors arising in the night after the great heat of the day. "When the Spaniards first landed in this country, they observed several villages built in the lake, which is the mode adopted by the Indians at present, [1810?] considering this plan the healthiest. The appearance of one of these little towns amid the waters, caused the Spanish adventurers to name it Little Venice, or Venezuela. Which title was afterwards transferred to the whole Province in the neighbourhood. "Four of these villages still remain [1810?] and are under the government of a monk, who has a church and the spiritual charge of the people."

and a landing made on February 23, 1528.[89b] Upon the following day, Dalfinger, with four hundred men and eighty horses, entered the native village of Coro,[90] unfurled the Imperial standard, and under its folds had himself acknowledged Governor and Captain-General of Welserland, the first German colony to be established in America, amid salvos of musketry and strains of martial music. A regular government was organized, a town projected and foundations were laid for a christian church,[90a] whose titular patron was St. Anna.[91]

---

[85] Karl von Klöden. Die Welser in Augsburg als besitzer von Venezuela, (Berlin, 1855), p. 437. Zeitschrift für Allgemeine Erdkunde, p. 437.

[86] Bartholomaeus Sailer, [Seyler] evidently a relation to Hieronymus Sailer and Johannes Sailer of Bamberg, for whom Johannes Schöner in 1520 constructed his celebrated globe. See above, p. 70.

[86a] He died during the last Dalfinger expedition, a few days before his commander.

[86b] These miners, all experienced men, were mainly from the St. Joachimsthal in the Erzgebirge. The negotiations were made by Hans Ehinger, who went to Joachimsthal for that purpose with Bergmeister Reiss and Jorg Neusesser, upon the part of the miners. After signing the contract the men were referred to Hieronymus Walther of Leipzig, who furnished the transportation to Seville.

[87] Geschichte der Welser-Züge in America, p. 42.

[88] Sebastian Rentz had previously travelled extensively through Asia and Africa in the interests of his employers the Welser Company, and as early as 1517 had obtained some reputation as a cartographer or map-maker.

[89] Not Governor of San Domingo, as stated by Weyermann.

[89b] Coro was chosen as a landing-place, because the pilots of that day were somewhat acquainted with that part of the coast; and further, there was a possibility of obtaining assistance there, if necessary, from the Europeans who were already in this vicinity.

[90] Originally an Indian village called Coriana. The first Europeans who landed here were a party of adventurers under Juan de Ampues,

Thus was established German civilization upon the soil of the new world, even prior to the Spanish conquest of Mexico or Peru.

The musical feature of the above celebration was undoubtedly the most inspiring part of the occasion. Historically it is the first record of an organized band of musicians in the new world. This is but another incident where the priority belongs to the German nation.

Many successive expeditions were sent out to America by the Germans after the edict was issued by Charles V, granting an extended permission to all of his German subjects to emigrate and settle in

---

who called the place Coro. Prior to the grant of the Germans, the whole territory was known as Coro. See Ternaux, introduction, pp. 4-5.

[90a] Dedicated July 26, 1529.

[91] Coro, or Santa Anna de Coro, afterwards became the capitol of Venezuela and the seat of the Spanish Viceroy. The town is situated at the head of a bay of the Gulf of Maracaibo, called El Golfete. It is built on several islands and a narrow sandy isthmus, which separates the gulf from the Caribbean sea. It is said that the original village found there by the Spaniards consisted of a group of houses built in the water upon piles, like those of the lake-dwellers. Recent explorations of the shell-mounds on the Florida Keys by Mr. Cushing have brought to light numerous remains which seem to indicate that this settlement upon the shore of Coro was a relic of an ancient civilization which once extended along the shores of the Caribbean sea and the Gulf of Mexico. Spanish records state that on acconut of the marine location of this Indian village, they called the place Little Venice, a name which eventually became Venezuela. During the Spanish *régime*, prior to 1636, the town was a rich and important one. After the removal of the seat of government to Caracas in the latter year, it lost much of its wealth and importance. It is now chiefly known for its commerce and export trade. The town has four fine churches and about 10,000 inhabitants. The great drawback to its development has been a lack of drinking water, which has to be carried from the mainland.

the West Indies. Among these expeditions of the Welsers which deserve special mention, are those

ARMS OF THE IMPERIAL CITY OF NURNBERG.

under Nicolaus Federmann, George Hohemuth,[92] von

---

[92] George Hohemuth (not Frohermuth, as occasionally written) was a native of Memmingen, but is usually known as of Speyer.

Speir, and the Frankish knight Philip von Hutten,[93] a nobleman from Birkenfeld; and, later, the expeditions sent out by the Fuggers to develop the western coast of South America.

---

[93] Philip von Hutten was a brother to Bishop Moritz von Hutten at Eichstedt. He left a diary covering the period from 1538 to 1541, which was published by Meusel, under the title *Zeitung aus Indien* (*Bibliotheca Historica*, vol. iii, lips., 1787).

## THE STORY OF WELSERLAND.

WELSER ARMS.

THE Welser expedition under Nicolaus Federmann, a native of Ulm, left San Lucar Barameda in Andalusia, on October 2, 1529, in a vessel supplied by Welser's agent, Ulrich Ehinger. The party consisted of 123 soldiers and twenty-four German miners [93a] (*Bergknappen*.) After a long and stormy voyage the adventurers reached San Domingo in December, 1529, and after refitting and obtaining the requisite number of horses, left for Coro. This expedition is of especial importance to us, as Federmann kept a careful account of his travels. This was published after his death by his kinsman, Hans Kifthaber of Ulm, in the year 1557. The only known copy of this book is in the Royal library at Stuttgart. It is a quarto of 122 pages ; following is the unique title and colophon :

"*Indianische Historia.* | *Ein schöne kurtz* | *weilige Historia Nicolaus Fe* | *dermanns des Jüngern von Ulm* | *erster raise so er von Hispania und* | *Andolosia auss in Indias des occea* | *nischen Mörs gethan hat, und* | *was ihm* | *allda ist begegnet biss auff sein widder-*

---

[93a] The contracts for this second contingent of German miners was made by Ulrich Ehinger, in the name of Bartholomaeus Welser, Ulrich Ehinger and their co-partners. The party was sent by Hieronymus Walther, of Leipzig. to Hamburg and Antwerp, whence they were transported by Welser's factors to Seville. Papers relating to this contract are still in existence. (*Kgl. Hauptstaatsarchiv.* Dresden.—Loc. 10428.) From which it appears that the party consisted of the following: Hans Trumpolt from Johannisthal; Velten (Valentin) Landhans (Landthans) from Zigenhals; Sigmunt Geppert (Gebhartt) from Wennsen; George Vnglaub (Jerg Vnglob) from Schwatz; Sixt Enderlin from Patmos; Wolf Dittrich (Wolff Dietrich) Freiberg; Merten Hoffmann from Altenberk; Wolf Gehe (Welff Gehe) from Kirchberg; Melcher Reuss from sant Annaberg; [st. Annaberg]; Niekel Teig (Nickell Legk) from Kempis; Critof Richter (Cristoff Richter) from the Neustadt; [Dresden?] Vrban Behm (Vrban Bohem) from Santa Annaberg; Moritz Putz (Putzlere) from Sneberg; Hanns Kestell, Burckhardt Ansorg, Hanns Weis, Hans Schick, Tomas Vogell, Hans Schenkel, two boys (names not given). The wife of Sigmunt Enderlein accompanied the party as a cook and washerwoman. She was presumably *the first German woman who put her foot upon American soil.* A number of these German miners not finding the new country to their liking, claimed they had been deceived and returned to their native country, where they arrived impoverished and disheartened. After their arrival in Saxony, they commenced judicial proceedings against all the parties connected with their enlistment. Many of the documents relating to this law suit are still preserved in the Royal Archives at Dresden.

*kunfft inn Hispaniam, auffs | kürtzete beschrieben, gantz | lustig zu lesen. | MDLVII. Getruckt zu Hagenaw bei Sigmund Bund.*"

On April 18, 1530, the colony was reinforced by

**Indianische Historia.**

In schöne kurtzweilige Historia Niclaus Federmanns des Jüngern von Ulm erster raise so er von Hispania biß Andolosia auß in Indias des Occeanischen Mörs gethan hat / und was ihm allda ist begegnet biß auff sein widerkunfft inn Hispaniam / auffs kurtzest beschriben / gantz lustig zu lesen.

M D · L V I I ·

TITLE PAGE OF FEDERMANN'S JOURNAL.
(Furnished by Prof. Th. Schott, Royal Librarian at Stuttgart.)

the arrival of three more vessels with colonists under command of Hans Seissenhoffer and George Ehinger.

The next important expedition to leave Europe was under the command of George Hohemuth von Speir, which left Spain on October 18, 1534, and arrived at Coro, February 5, 1535. This party consisted of over 600 adventurers. Among the officers were Philip von Hutten,[94] a nobleman from Birkenfeld; Hieronymus Köller from Nürnberg; Majordomus Andreas Gundelfinger, Paymaster Franz Lebzelter from Ulm; Nicolaus Federmann and Hans Vöhlin from Augsburg, the last a nephew of the Welsers.[95]

Among the adventurers sent out there was a band of eighteen musicians, together with a number of artisans. Special mention is made of a printer [95a] (*Buchdrucker*), evidently bringing with him a printing press and type. This is the earliest record of any printer having been sent to America. Unfortunately, beyond the mere mention in the official list, that a printer was sent out among the craftsmen who went in this expedition, there is nothing to show, either in the way of an imprint or documentary evidence, that he ever did any printing in America, or that a press was even established at Coro.

Should, however, any imprint of this hitherto unknown printer ever come to light, it may prove to be a German one printed with German type: it could

---

[94] In Spanish records Philip *de Urre, Uten, Utre, Urra*, etc.
[95] See foot-note, p. 71 *supra*.
[95a] Geschichte der Welser-Züge, p. 94.

## Founding of Bogota.

but antedate by a few years the known imprints of Jakob Cromberger of 1540 without in the least affecting the fact that to the German nation is due the honor of establishing the printing press in the western world.

It is not within the scope of this paper to follow up the various expeditions undertaken during the next quarter of a century by the Germans, which extended hundreds of miles into the interior of South America, to relate how the city of Bogota was founded early in 1539, by Nicolaus Federmann during his second expedition, a city which is now the capital of the United States of Colombia. Nor will we recite the sufferings of these brave adventurers, or chronicle their deeds; how brave Ambrose Dalfinger died the death of a hero,[96] or the lamented George von Speir fell a victim to the tropical fever.[97] It would fill several volumes to do justice to this epoch in American history. Suffice it to say that the successive expeditions under Dalfinger, Sailer,[98] Federmann, Ehinger, Sarmiento, Alemann,[99] Seissenhoffer, Hohemuth, Heinrich Rembold and Hutten,[100] tended to

---

[96] According to Weyland, Dalfinger was wounded by the natives in 1531, in a valley about six hours from Pampelona. This spot still bears the name *Vale de Micer* (Mister or Herr) *Ambrosio*. He died about a week later at the deserted village of Chinacota where he was buried. See Geschichte der Welser-Züge, p. 84-5.

[97] Also called George Spirra. His various expeditions into the interior extended over a period of five years. He returned to San Domingo in 1539, where he shortly afterwards died.

[98] After the death of Dalfinger, Lieutenant Bartholomaeus Sailer succeeded to the command of the Colony. He, however, also died in 1532, a short time after his superior.

settle and develop the unknown wilds of tropical America, even if they did fail to bring their projectors the coveted golden reward.

The Germans in America, however, had a worse enemy to contend with than tropical fever, poisoned arrows or treacherous elements. This was the jealousy of the Spaniard, to whom, after the religious peace of Nürnberg, all Germans appeared as Lutherans and heretics. No opportunity was left pass, when anything detrimental could be done to the Germans: at Court, in Spain, as well as in America, it was always the same story.

Unfortunately the history of this first attempt at German colonization in America closes with a double tragedy—the brutal murder of the chivalrous Philip von Hutten,[101] Captain General of Welserland, and

---

[99] Juan Aleman, Johannes der *Teutsche*, John, the German. The identity of this German adventurer is shrouded in more or less mystery. Weyland, in his history of Venezuela, wherein he follows Depons and Oviedo, states that Johannes, a German, was sent out by the Welser Company to seize the government of the colony in the event of Alfinger's death. The account goes on to state that, either on account of the devastation wrought by Dalfinger in his expeditions, or else through lack of courage, Johannes is said never to have left Coro.

[100] The names of Melchior Grübel (arms on page 75) and Meister Hans Kistler aus Geldern also occupy a prominent place in the history of German enterprise in South America.

[101] Philip von Hutten (Philip von de Urre) spent over fifteen years in Venezuela, most of the time in exploring and developing the country and its resources. He was also a firm believer in the existence of an El-Dorado in the interior, and led several expeditions with the object of finding and conquering that mythical land of gold. His greatest feat was when he, together with 39 German soldiers, fought and defeated over 15,000 Omegas. See Weyland, *Reise in Terra Firma*, (Berlin, 1808,) pp. 282, *et seq.*

CONTEMPORARY MAP SHOWING POSSESSIONS OF THE WELSER
COMPANY IN SOUTH AMERICA.

(ORIGINAL IN THE UNIVERSITY LIBRARY AT BOLOGNA.)

## Murder of the German Commanders. 101

Bartolomaeus Welser, eldest son of the senior member of the great Augsburg firm, who, in 1541, had been sent to Welserland as Governor. The Spanish records call him "*Don Bartolomeo Belzar, Gobernador de su Majestad, Adelantado del Reino de Venezuela.*"[101a]

PHILIP VON HUTTEN.

The two German commanders were murdered on April 18, 1546, by order of the Spaniard, Caravajal.[102] When the news of this tragedy reached Germany it caused great indignation, which even the summary execution of Caravajal failed to assuage.

The Welsers, from now onward, took less interest

---

[101a] Hutten, in his diary, writes under date of March 10, 1541: "Vor kurzen Tagen ist Herrn Bartolma Welser's Sohn hier angekommen, ein verständiger junger Gesell, über dessen Ankunft alle grosse Freude gehabt haben ; ich habe keinen Zweifel dass ihn die Herrn Welser zum Gubernator machen werden, da Gott ihn zu solcher Zeit geschickt hat."

[102] Juan de Caravajal accompanied as notary the first Welser expedition to America, which was sent out under Dalfinger. He afterwards returned to San Domingo, where it appears he remained until 1542. After the death of Heinrich Rembold (1542), he was sent to Coro to take charge of the Government in the absence of Philip von Hutten, Imperial Captain-General, and young Welser, who were upon an extended expedition in the interior. Caravajal at once assumed charge of affairs at Coro, and upon learning that the Germans had experienced great hardships and were returning in a shattered condition, and that the troops were weakened from wounds and disease, he, at the instiga-

in the development of their possessions in South America.[102b] They still, however, held the title and a dominating influence in its affairs for another decade, as it was not until the year 1555 that they were finally debarred from their concessions for some unexplained reason, after an exasperating law-suit which was decided against them.[103] Thus ended the first organized scheme of German colonization in America.[104]

---

tion of Pedro de Limpias, attempted to secure control of the government and combine the colony with that of New Granada. Caravajal, with a number of Spaniards, rode out to meet the returning Germans. Hutten and Welser, who suspected no treachery, were seized while their men were out foraging, and at once executed under an old tree, which still stands in the plaza of Tocuyo. The two Germans were beheaded by a negro with a dull hunting-knife. Some of the German troops escaped to Coro, where in the meantime Juan Perez de Tolosa had arrived, bearing special concessions from the Crown. As soon as he was informed of Caravajal's treachery, he ordered him to be taken to the spot and executed in a similar manner.

[102b] From the Welser Codex in the British Museum, it appears that the attempts to dispossess the Germans of their possessions in America commenced as early as May 11, 1535, with an instruction sent out by the Queen regent to Bishop Bastidas, wherein she implores him to keep a watchful eye upon the German colonists in his Province, (Venezuela) as it has been stated that a number of persons emigrated to the new country without complying with the published statutes, not only to the prejudice of the Spanish character of the country, but above all endangering the unity and purity of the faith. All such cases were to be reported direct to Seville at once without delay, and such persons [evidently who professed the Lutheran faith] were to be banished forthwith.

[103] Antheil der Deutschen an der EntdeckungAmerikas. (Stuttgart, 1857.)

[104] There are still a number of families in Venezuela who trace their ancestry to some of the German adventurers of Welserland. In many cases it is a source of pride, not even surpassed by that of the Spanish grandees.

The question will undoubtedly arise in the minds of many persons, why this epoch in German and American history has not been brought out with the prominence which it deserves? The answer is that most of the accounts bearing upon the subject are stored in the archives at Seville, wherein the long-forgotten actors are lost under Hispanicized and foreign names;[105] and such poets as sung the Germans' praises in their epic poems[106] have long been cast aside as strains that grate harshly upon the jealous Spanish ear.[107]

The usually accepted account of the German regime in America is that of the Dominican monk las Casas,[108] who in his work on the Indies, "*Tyran-*

---

[105] In Spanish and Portuguese records, the German name of Welser is variously changed to Velseri, Berzer, Berzares, Belzares, Belzaras, Bersyrs, Belsyres, etc., while the Fuggers appear as Fucares, Folkyres, Fouchers, etc. Amerkungen zur Geschichte der Welser-Züge, p. 297.

[106] Poems of Juan de Castellanos. *Primera parte de las Elegias de varones ilustres de Indias, compuestas por Juan de Castellanos, etc.* (Madrid, 1589.) See Ticknor, History of Spanish Literature (London, 1863,) ii, p. 472. Volume ii, of Castellanos contains the Welser episode.

[107] Hermann A. Schumacher, in Hamburger Fest-schrift, vol. ii, p. 227.

[108] Bartholomew de las Casas, a Spanish prelate, was born at Seville 1474, and in his nineteenth year accompanied his father, who sailed with Columbus to the West Indies. Five years afterward he returned to Spain, and pursuing his studies, entered the ecclesiastical order. He again accompanied Columbus in his second voyage to Hispaniola, and on the conquest of Cuba settled there, and distinguished himself by his humane conduct toward the oppressed natives, of whom he became in a manner the patron saint. In 1516 he returned to Europe to state the case of the Indians before the Crown. The regent Ximenes appointed a commission to investigate the charges. The outcome of this investigation not meeting with his approbation, he again went to Spain to lay the case of the Indians before the new King and Emperor Charles V.

nies et cruautez des Espagnols, commises es Indes Occidentales, qu' on dit le Noveau Monde," in the chapter on Venezuela accuses the Germans (whom he called Flemings) [109] of the greatest barbarities and cruelty, beside which even the tortures of the Inquisition sink into insignificance.

There is, however, a twofold explanation of this unjust criticism of the German pioneers. The first is to be found in the national jealousy that was then so strong between the two nations. The other one, the religious feature, arose from the fact that the Germans were accused of introducing the Lutheran religion into the colony. It is difficult to say just what proof there is of this charge. According to v. Klöden the entire German contingent in South America as early as 1532 had accepted the Lutheran faith.[109b]

Certain it is, however, that the brave Philip von

---

Las Casas, by a singular inconsistency, in his zeal for the Indians, became the author of the slave-trade, by proposing to purchase negroes from the Portuguese in Africa to supply the planters with laborers, of the want of whom they complained; a proposition which was unfortunately put into execution. His famous *Brevissima Relacion de la Destruccion des Indies* is well known. So far as the charges of cruelty against the Germans are concerned, they seem to have been inspired mainly by the fact that von Hutten and others refused to attend mass. In short he calls the Germans heretics and Lutherans. Las Casas afterwards became Bishop of Chiapa. He eventually fell into disfavor with his superiors, lost his bishopric, and died in comparative obscurity in Madrid in 1556, in the 92nd year of his age. To such as know nothing of his inconsistency in regard to the negro, he generally appears as a benevolent character, whose chief aim in life was the relief of the oppressed aborigines in the West Indies.

[109] Spanish Edition Paris MDCXCVII pp. 115 *et seq.*

Hutten refused to attend mass, even if he was not an avowed Lutheran. Las Casas further states: The Flemish General [v. Hutten] is nothing but a heretic; he never attends mass himself, nor suffers others to go, and he further shows plain evidences of Lutheranism, whereby one may know him.[109c]

Then again there are three arguments, which controvert the trustworthiness of the Las Casas account:[110]

1. He fails to name any one of the German Governors whom he accuses of gross cruelty toward the natives.

2. The accounts are evidently aimed at Ambrose Dalfinger, who was charged with every type of barbarity actually committed by native Spaniards in the adjoining provinces.

3. No charge of cruelty whatsoever can be brought against either Johann the German (Johann Alemann), or Philip v. Hutten. George von Speir was only exceptionally harsh when occasion required it, and even Federmann, the soldier of fortune, ever inclined toward mercy and humanity.[111]

It certainly seems somewhat anomalous for a

---

[109b] If this be so then we may claim that date as the introduction of the Lutheran faith into the western world. (*Die Welser in Augsburg als besitzer von Venezuela*, p. 440.)

[109c] Las Casas: Die Verheerung West Indiens. German edition (Berlin, 1790) pp. 146-7. Also, *Relacion de la destruccion de las Indias Occidentalis. Presentado a' Felipe* ii. (Philadelphia, 1821,) Chap. *Reyno de Venezuela*, pp. 109-117.

[110] These charges of Las Casas were publicly contradicted at the time by Sepulveda, of Cordova, who was the official historiographer of the Emperor Charles V. Rome 15—.

bishop of the order that introduced the Tribunal of the Inquisition into the world, and who was the original instigator of negro slavery in America, to charge the Germans in America with any such inhumanity.

Further, according to the lately discovered Welser-Codex in the British Museum, the fact is proven beyond any doubt, that the treatment of the Indians in Venezuela by the Germans, was no more cruel there than elsewhere. On the contrary, all indications point to a policy of friendly intercourse between the Germans and the Indians. Consequently, notwithstanding the implied permission enjoyed by the Germans for maintaining a slave-trade, the condition of the Venezuela Indians was by no means so bad as

ARMS OF THE REPUBLIC OF VENEZUELA.

to justify the charges made against the Germans by Las Casas. This fact is fully set forth in the above original document.[111a]

---

[111] Karl Klunzinger, Antheil der Deutschen an der Entdeckung Sud Americas. (Stuttgart, 1857,) p. 111.
[111a] Der Welser-Codex, see foot note 77a *supra*.

## THE GRANTS TO ANTON AND HIERONYMUS FUGGER.

THE FUGGER ARMS.

THE ACCOUNTS of the grant made by Charles V. to Anton and Hieronymus Raimond Fugger, merchants and bankers at Augsburg, are not quite so clear, as the documents bearing upon the transaction were stored in the archives at Seville, and during the past centuries, like many similar ones, have long since been forgotten.

Lately, however, a number of these papers, bearing upon the exploration and settlement of the west coast of South America, were resurrected, examined

THE "FUGGER" HOUSE AT AUGSBURG.

THE MURAL PAINTINGS UPON THE FRONT ILLUSTRATE THE HISTORY OF THE FAMILY DURING REIGN OF CHARLES V.
(FROM PHOTOGRAPH FURNISHED BY STADTARCHIVAR HERR ADOLF BUFF.)

and published by Senor J. T. Medina.[112]  *Coleccion de documentas ineditos para la historia de Chili, Tom. III.*

From these records it appears that the grant to the Fugger firm embraced the whole lower end of the southern hemisphere, between the straits of Magellan and the southern boundary of Peru;[113] in fact, that Chili, the most progressive of the modern republics of South America, was originally a German colony.

HIERONYM. FUGGER

From these documents as published it appears that the original grant was made on July 25, 1529, to one Simon de Aleazaba. It was not long, however, before we find the concession transferred to the Germans; Veit Hörl,[114] the resident factor of the Fuggers at Seville, having negotiated the transfer.[115]

There appears to have been considerable negotiation between the Spanish Indian office and the German merchants in reference to the particulars and emoluments. A personal

---

[112] Zeitschrift der Geselschaft für Erdkunde zu Berlin. Vol. xxvii, p. 407.

[113] The concession mentions the stretch of coast extending 200 leguas from the west cape of the straits of Magalhen, to the District of Chincha,

appeal to the Emperor by one of the German merchants, however, settled the dispute in their favor. One of the conditions of the grant was that the Fuggers were to send out three expeditions, with no less than 500 men, to take possession and explore the country. The same powers vested in the Welsers were conferred upon them. The German firm had the right of appointment of all officers from Captain-General downward. The governorship of the colony was to be hereditary for three generations, counting Anton Fugger as the first one. This grant also secured to the Fuggers the monopoly of all trade within the bounds of the Province.

It appears that the Fuggers were very exacting in their demands upon the Emperor as to the particulars of the colonial Government. A demand which was imperatively insisted upon was one that should forever redound to the honor of the noble German house who refused to accept the charter unless it contained a provision against the system of enslaving the natives, known as *encomiendas*.

The Fuggers not only demanded that Charles V.

---

which was the southernmost point of the grant made to Pizarro. *Ibid* p. 408. See also "Die Fugger and der Spanische Gewürzhandel." Augsburg 1892.

[114] In the Spanish documents, this factor appears as Guido Herl, Hezerle or Horrelo. According to the "Personal Repertorium" of the family archives of the noble Fugger family, the correct name is Veit Hörl. Here is also preserved his last will and testament, together with a document wherein Hörl endowed a charitable institution in the year 1546. See also K. Heabler. Zeitschrift, vol xxvii. Berlin, 1892.

[115] *Ibid*, pp. 111-112.

## The Earliest Protest against Slavery. 111

should abstain from granting any *encomienda*[116] privileges within the bounds of their province, but also undertook, so far as they were concerned, to accept the provision against this form of slavery in its fullest sense. They were evidently satisfied as to the iniquity of the institution, and that in their opinion other and more humane means would be found to further the colonization of the colony and the civilization of the Indians far more rapidly than could be done by means of servitude.[117] We have here a German protest against human slavery which antedates the celebrated Germantown one by fully a century and a half.[118] It was well toward the end of 1531 ere the negotiations were ended, and the document signed by the Spaniards upon one part, and Veit Hörl, as agent for his principals, upon the other.

ANTONIUS FUGGER
Comes et Consiliar. Cæs.

---

[118] Weyland (Berlin, 1808,) who endorsed this system of slavery, (p. 43) gives the following description of the system known in Spanish annals as *Encomiendas*. He states that the object of the system was to bring all Indians within a certain district under the supervision of some intelligent Spaniard, without, however, conferring upon him any absolute right of possession (Eigenthumsrecht.) He was required: 1. To pro-

Another interesting feature of the concession granted to the Fugger company by Charles V. was the right and privilege to mint and coin both gold and silver money, for circulation at home as well as in the provinces granted them.

Thus far no accounts have been published as to the expeditions sent out to Chili, or what efforts, if

---

tect them from all imposition and oppression, to which they were liable by reason of their ignorance of the requirements of the civil laws. 2. To unite them in one village, without, however, being permitted to live among them. 3. To cause them to be instructed in the Christian religion. 4. To regulate their social economy, and obtain the respect for the heads of families due them, a condition entirely unknown to the Indians 5. To observe the relationship in the various families, and to introduce such customs as would bring about civilized order. 6. To instruct them in agriculture, and such trades as would be of benefit to them. 7. To eradicate all desires or customs of their former savage mode of life.

For the above endeavors in their behalf, these Encomiendas, as the Indians were now called, were required to pay their Master or Encomenderos, a yearly tribute, either in manual labor, in the products of the ground, or in money. (Weyland, pp. 43-5. See, also Mitchell's translation of Depons Voyage to Terra Firma.) The tribute, perhaps in most cases, required not only the labor of the head of the family, but of every man, woman and child as well. It was merely a cloak for the worst kind of slavery. The Indians were parcelled out by thousands by the Court of Spain to the various favorites, both male and female. There were Encomenderos who never came to America, but collected their tribute by proxy through resident agents, who, if their demands were not paid, simply sold the Indians into absolute slavery in adjoining colonies. The law permitting this terrible abuse of the American natives was abrogated in 1568. See also Zeitschrift der Gesellschaft für Erdkunde zu Berlin, Band XXVII, 1892, pp. 405-419.

[117] Haebler, Kolonial Unternehmungen der Fugger, (Berlin, 1892) p. 417.

[118] Done at Germantown, Pennsylvania: "Ye 18 of the 2 month 1688." For text in full see Pennypacker's Historical and Biographical sketches. Philadelphia 1883, pp. 42-45.

any, were made by the Germans at colonization on the western coast of America.

Before passing the subject of German activity in the development of South America, we will state that the Germans did not confine their attention alone to the north and west coast of the new hemisphere, but were equally active in the exploration of Brazil and the countries adjacent to the Rio de la Platte. Here again the name and enterprise of the Welsers and other German merchants are met with, more or less prominently. Two printed accounts have come down to us of the exploration and settlement of the countries now known as Paraguay and Buenos Ayres, which show how the Germans shared in the vicissitudes of their early settlement.

The most prominent of these books is the Narrative of Ulrich Schmidt von Straubingen,[119] a native of Bavaria, and covers the period from 1534-1554. It gives an account of how he went upon an expedition to America in one of the Welser vessels. This was published at Frankfort——by Sebastian Franck and Sigismund Feyerabend, in a collection of Voyages, under the following title:[120]

"*Warhafftige vnd liebliche Beschreibung etlicher fürnemen Indianischen Landschafften vnd Insulen, die vormals in keiner Chronicken gedacht, vnd erstlich in der Schiffart Vlrici Schmidts von Straubingen, mit*

---

[119] Known in Spanish records as "*Schmidel*" and "*Uldericus Faber*."
[120] An English translation of this book has lately been published by the Hakluyt Society. "The conquest of the River Platte, 1535-1555." London 1891.

*grosser gefahr erkundigt, vnd von ihm selber auffs fleissigst beschrieben vnd dargethan.* MDLXVII.

The other work is the narrative of Hans Stade and covers the period 1547-1554.[120a]

Warachti | ge Historie ende be | schrivinge eens landts in America ghelegen, wiens inwoonders wilt, | naeckt, seer godloos, ende Wreede | Menschen eters sijn. Beschreuen door Hans Staden van Homborch ut lant van | Hessen, die welcke seluer in Persoone | het landt America besocht heeft. | Vt den Hoochduysch-overgheset. | Tantwerpen | By Christoffel Plantyn, unde gulden Eenhooren. 1558 Met privilgif. |

ARMS OF THE REPUBLIC OF CHILI.

---

[120a] Copies of both the above rare volumes are in the Carter Brown Library, Providence, R. I.

## RELIGIOUS CAUSES INDUCIVE TO GERMAN EMIGRATION.

FAC-SIMILE OF THE TITLE PAGE OF BROADSIDE CORT-UNY, THE FRUEHN ARTICLE OF THE PEASANTS, A. D., 1525.

RETURNing once more to the period of the Reformation, two other historical episodes are recalled, which in the course of a century and a half were destined to exercise considerable influence upon the exodus of the Germans from the Fatherland, and the future complexion of our Commonwealth. The first of these movements, the so-called Peasants' War (1524-26) was an uprising of the masses in central and southern Germany in the interests of a universal democracy. It ended in their defeat and an increase of the burdens of the peasantry, and we may say their further enslavement.

The other episode, a religious movement, under

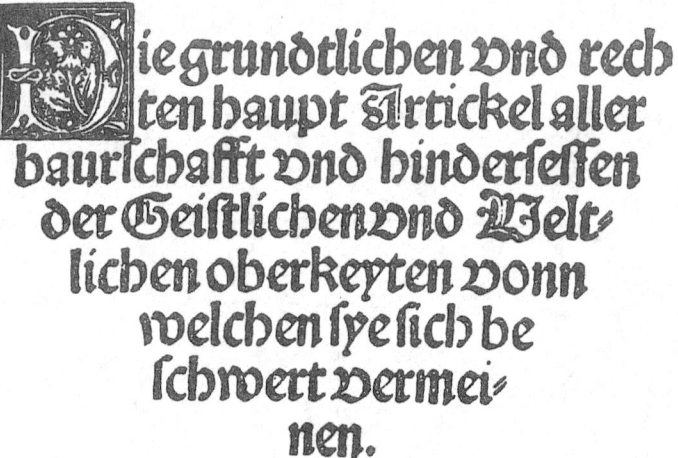

TITLE PAGE OF THE TWELVE ARTICLES OF 1525.

the leadership of Knipperdolling and Johann von Leydere, called by various names, most generally "Anabaptist"[120b] (1519-1534) though small at first and accompanied by the wildest excesses of lawless fanaticism,[121] in the course of years, under the teach-

---

[120b] The Anabaptist movement in Germany was in reality an outcome of the Peasants' war. The chief seat of this agitation was at Münster in Westphalen, where under the leadership of Knipperdolling and his son-in-law John of Leyden, both the religious and civil government was assumed by the adherents of the new sect.

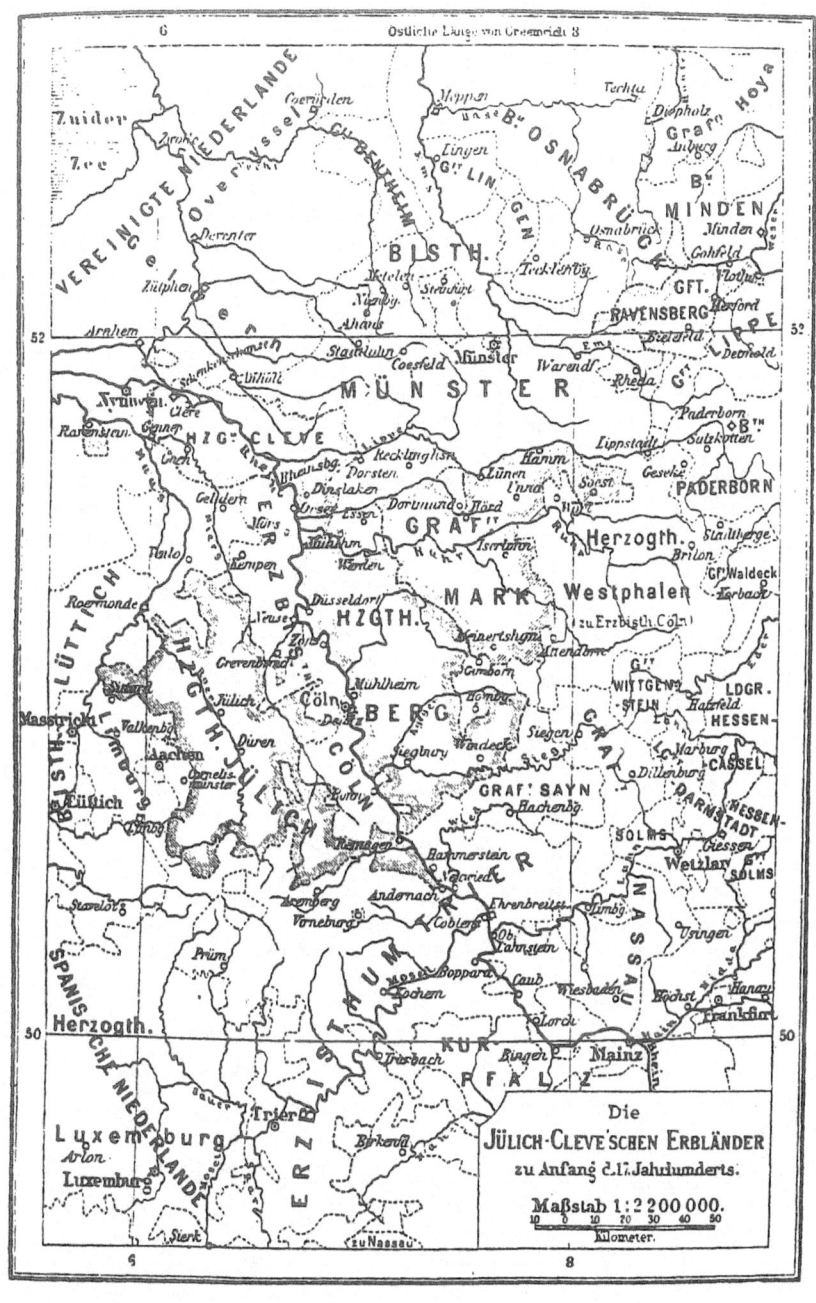

The JÜLICH-CLEVE Hereditary Domain at the commencement
of the XVIIth Century.

# Ain Sermon geprediget vom
Pawren zů Werdt/bey Nürmberg/am Sontag
vor Faßnacht/von dem freyen willen
des menschen/auch von anrůf-
fung der hailigen.

TITLE PAGE OF BROADSIDE CIRCULATED AMONG THE PEASANTRY.

ings of Menno Simon, who gathered up the scattered Baptists, resolved itself into the denominations known as Mennonites, Dunkers and similar congregations, who are now among our most peaceful and harmless Christians. Their haven of rest was eventual'y found in the fertile valleys of our own Pennsylvania,[122] and their descendants are to-day among our most thrifty and respected citizens.

TITLE OF THE FIRST GERMAN BIBLE.
(Reduced Fac-Simile.)

---

[121] The main cause for these excesses was a certain Johannes Bockhold, a tailor of Leyden, who came to Münster in 1533. Assuming the name of John of Leyden, he excited a portion of the populace, and had himself declared as king of New Zion. From this period 1534, Münster became the theatre of all the excesses of fanaticism, lust and cruelty. The city was captured June 24, 1535, by the forces under the Bishop of Münster, and the kingdom of the Anabaptists was destroyed by the execution of the chief men.

In the year 1520, while the emperor Charles V. was sojourning in Germany, a letter was handed to him from America. This missive, dated July 16, 1519, and now in the archives of the Imperial Library at Vienna, was from Hernando Cortez, and told of the capture of a country rich in precious ore. This was welcome news to that impecunious ruler. The returns for the next decade, however, failed to make any great impression upon the finances of Spain, and it was not until the stream of blood-stained gold from Peru reached Spain in 1534, that the emperor of Germany and king of Spain felt himself free from the power of the German merchants, and in a position to curtail the privileges of these wealthy commercial corporations, the chief among which was the powerful Hanseatic League, whose influence had so long excited the jealousy of the German emperor and his electors.

This improvement in Spain's finances and their consequent independence of German merchants, was followed by a cloud of Latin bigotry and intolerance, which again darkened the horizon of the Fatherland and threatened to sweep away the last vestige of religious liberty obtained after so severe a struggle at the Peace of Nürnberg in 1532.

The Council of Trent (1545) had become a matter of history. Charles V, being then free from foreign complications and acting under the impulses of the

---

[122] See Mennonite Emigration to Pennsylvania, by Dr. J. G. DeHoop Scheffer, Amsterdam, in Penna. Magazine of History. Vol. ii p. 117.

Council, with the flood of silver at his disposal, which was now coming in by the cargo, being the output of the mines of Potosi, determined to make a mighty effort to crush the independence of the estates of the empire in Germany and the Protestant religion at the same time. He was urged on by the Pope, Paul III, who sent a contingent of 12,000 foot and 1,000 horse. Charles V, in his ambition, however, was opposed by the so-called Schmalkaldic League,[123] a confederation of the Protestant princes and imperial cities under the leadership of John Frederick, of Saxony. A two-years' war was the result, and ended disastrously for the Protestants.[124]

These troubles did not come to an end until September 25, 1555, when the religious peace of Augsburg[125] was consummated. But this only granted religious freedom to such as adhered to the Augsburg Confession. It secured no privileges whatever to the Reformed (Geneva) religion.

---

[123] The Smalcaldic League was concluded February, 27, 1531, by 7 Princes, 2 Counts and 11 free cities for mutual defence of their religious and political independence against Charles V. and the Catholic States.

[124] The victory of the Imperial forces over Philip von Hessen, at Mühlberg, April 24, 1547.

[125] The territorial princes and the free cities, who, at this date, acknowledged the confession of Augsburg, received freedom of worship, the right to introduce the reformation within their territories (*jus reformandi*), and equal rights with the Catholic estates. No agreement reached as regarded the Ecclesiastical Reservation (*Reservatum ecclesiasticum*) that the spiritual estates (bishops and abbots) who became Protestant should lose their offices and incomes. This peace secured no privileges for the Reformed (Geneva) religion.

This state of religious intolerance and unrest in both Germany and France culminated during the memorable year of 1555 in an attempt being made to establish a distinctively Protestant settlement in America. It was made under the patronage of Admiral de Coligny, but failed through the defection of the leader.[126] In 1562 and 1564 a second and third attempt were made under the same auspices. These latter ventures were within the bounds of the United States, and among the emigrants were a number of Alsatians and Hessians who had served under the Admiral's brother.

The settlement in 1562 was made near Port Royal in South Carolina, and was soon abandoned. Two years later Coligny sent out an expedition under René Laudonniere to carry aid and reinforcements to Ribault's colony. Finding the settlement abandoned, they sailed up the St. John's river in Florida, and there built Fort Carolina. Ribault arrived the following year, August 28, 1565. Three weeks later the settlement was captured by Spaniards under Mendez de Aviles, who had all the settlers brutally tortured and murdered; after which he set up a placard: "*I do this not as to Frenchmen, but as to Lutherans.*" Ribault, with a number of settlers, escaped to sea, but his vessel was wrecked, and the crew and company shared the same fate as their fellows at Fort Carolina.

In Germany the era of religious tranquillity proved

---

[126] Chevalier Nicolaus Durand de Villegegannon.

of but short duration. The abdication of Emperor Charles V, January 15, 1556, at Brussels; the election of his younger brother (Ferdinand I, 1556-1564) and the reign of the latter's son, Maximilian II, 1564-1576, and grandson, Rudolph II, 1576-1612, (a learned man who fostered the occult sciences, and was an adept in astrology, alchemy and astronomy) all happened within a quarter of a century. Then came a reaction against Protestantism, which led to the formation of a Protestant Union (1608) under Frederick IV, elector Palatine; and a Catholic Union a year later, led by Maximilian, duke of Bavaria.[127] To further complicate matters, Rudolph II was succeeded by his childless brother, Matthias (1612-1619.) The latter having obtained the renunciation of his brothers, secured the imperial succession for his cousin Ferdinand, duke of Styria, (Ferdinand II, 1619-1637) who had been educated by the Jesuits in strict Catholicism. The outcome of these various complications was the great struggle known in history as the Thirty Years' War.[128]

This struggle is generally divided into four periods, which were really as many different wars. The first two, known as the Bohemian and Danish, had a predominant religious character; they developed from

---

[127] Both of the above leaders were princes of the house of Wittelsbach.

[128] The various rulers of Europe at the outbreak of this celebrated struggle were: Emperor, Matthias; Pope, Paul V; Sultan, Osman; Spain, Naples and Sicily, Philip III; France, Louis XIII; England, James I; Poland, Sigismundus III; Denmark and Norway, Christian IV; Sweden, Gustavus Adolphus; Bohemia, Ferdinand II; Hungary, Ferdinand.

Zeitung auß Cöln/ vom 18. Junij. Anno 1609.

Auß dem Hage wirdt mit den letsten Brieffen anders nichts geschrieben/ dann daß die Frantzösische vnnd Englische Gesanden daselbst nunmehr bereitschafft machen/ersten tages wider nach Hauß zuziehen. Sonst hett so wol/ der Ertzhertzog als die Herrn Staden ein gute anzahl Kriegsvolck abgedanckt/ vnd sie vollends bezahlen lassen. Es schreiben die von Ambsterdam/daß die Kauffhandlung vnd Nahrung/daselbst vnd ander orten wegen dieses anstands täglich abnemen/ vornemlich/ weil sich jetzt so viel Meerräuber uff dem Meer erzeigen/welche immer die Kauffahrende Schiff plundern/vnnd theils gar zu sich nemen/ wie dann auch wegen deß jetzigen Kriegswesen zwischen Schweden/Polen vnd Mosscaw die handlung auß Holl: vnd Seeland nach den orteen auch nit dann mit grosser gefahr geschehen könne. Brieff auß Louden melden/ daß die Flotta mit 8 Schiffen/ mit viel Manns vnnd Weibspersohnen sampt anderer *provision*, vmb das Land Virginia Volckreich vnd wohnhafft zumachen/dahin abgesegelt sein/mit grossem mißfall der Spannier. Beyde Fürsten von Brandenburg vnd Newburg/ haben sich zu Dortmund vnder einander/ durch nittel Landgraff Moritzen dahin verglichen/daß sie gegen alle andere anmassungen zu erhaltung vnd *defension* der Gülischen Lande zusamen setzen/ vnd innerhalb 4. Monaten sich allerdings dahin vergleichen sollen/wer der rechte Erb dieser Landen sein wird/vnnd sollen ihn in mittelst von den Stenden etliche zugeordnet werden/ vmb die Regierung/ biß zu besserer bestellung zu *continuiren*, auch mit deß Fürsten Begräbnuß fort fahren/ vnnd sonsten weiters zu verordnen/was der sachen zum besten dieser Landen erfordern wird/darauff obgedachte beede Fürsten zu Düsseldorff angelangt sein/wiewol sich die gewesene Gülische Rähte noch dargegen gesetzt/ aber durch die Burger gleichwol eingelassen worden/ vnd auffs Schloß ziehen lassen/was nun weiters folgen wird/gibt zeit.

Auß Rom/ vom 30. May.

Demnach der *Pater Spinola* ein Jesuiter/ so deß Cardinals *Spinola* Bruder ist/ auß den Orientalischen Indien/alda er seither Bapsts Gregorij deß 13. Lebzeiten bey 30. Jahren gewest/ alher kommen/hat er Sontags beym Bapst *Audienz* gehabt/in welcher er demselben *referirt*, wie die Römische Religion der orten stets zuneme/ auch viel wunderliche sachen *præsentirt*. Die Malthesische vnd Neapolitanische Galleren sind mit einander in *Compagnia* außgefahren/ die *reveriren* daß Königreichs Neapoli vmbzuschiffen/ es ist auch der Oerten den reisigen befehl zukommen/sich mit der Landschafft besatzung in bereitschafft finden zulassen/damit auff 24. Junij jede *Compagnia* an bestimpten ort sich einstellen möge. Weil man *Aviso*, daß die Türckische Galleren vnd Vasellen von *Thunis* außgefahren/ also wirdt besorgt/ sie möchten in Romagna einfallen/deßwegen solches zuverhüten/ hat man etlich 100. Soldaten zur *Quardia* dahin geschickt/ auch dem *Signor Ioan del fale Obersten* vber dieselbe Provinz vom General
Fran-

Fac-simile page from the oldest known German newspaper.
It contains a notice of an expedition to Virginia.

the revolt in Bohemia to a general attack by Catholic Europe upon Protestant Europe. The last two wars, the Swedish and Swedish-French were political wars; wars against the power of the house of Hapsburg, and wars of conquest on the part of Sweden and France upon German soil.

## THE THIRTY YEARS' WAR.

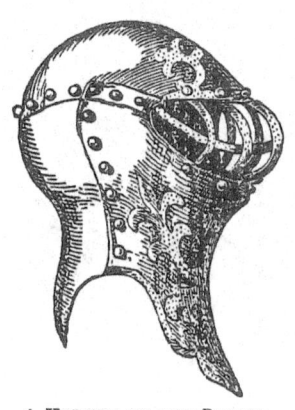

A Helmet of the Period.

NEVER IN THE HIStory of Germany, since it occupied a place among civilized nations, did the Fatherland present so lamentable and helpless a condition as was the case during the second half of the XVIIth century, after the terrors of the great war were over.

The actual damage entailed by the extended struggle known as the Thirty Years' War is hard to estimate. Perhaps the greatest real harm done to the nation was the breaking down of almost every barrier of moral or religious restraint; a condition which led, more or less, to the abandonment of all the ties of domestic life.[129]

The actual losses of Germany during this period of devastation can only be approximated by consult-

THE PENNSYLVANIA-GERMAN SOCIETY.

MEDAL COMMEMORATING THE PEACE OF WESTPHALIA.

DISK OF SILVER.
THIRTY-EIGHT SIXTEENTHS OF AN INCH IN DIAMETER.

(ORIGINAL IN POSSESSION OF
MR. HARRY ROGERS, PHILADELPHIA.)

ing the statistics of individual states or communities. Thus in Würtemberg, from 1634-41 over 345,000 human beings perished by sword, famine and pestilence, and at the close of the war the Duchy had but 48,000 inhabitants, impoverished and disheartened. Eight cities, 45 villages, 65 churches, and 158 school and parochial houses had been burned. Before the war the Palatinate was credited with a population of half a million souls; at the close of the struggle, a census showed less than one-tenth of the original number.

Perhaps the most drastic and yet not overdrawn description of Germany's condition is given by Scherr in his *Cultur und Sittengeschichte*, wherein he states: "The scum of Europe's mercenary hirelings spread over Germany's fertile plains, and there perpetrated the most terrible martial tragedy which has ever been recorded upon pages in the history of nations."

To the nameless licentiousness of the military customs of that day must be added a repulsive sentimentality combined with inhumanity, and an insane desire to kill for the mere pleasure of murdering.

The countless cases of arson, robbery and homicide, the slaughter of innocent children, the rape of maiden and matron, often in view of the helpless parent or father, who had been previously bound, maimed or mutilated; the massacre of the population of entire towns which had been captured; the drenching of the populace with a villainous

---

[129] Ursprung und wesen des Pietismus. Sachsse, Wiesbaden, 1884.

A Camp Scene During the Thirty Years' War.
(The Portable Prison in the Left Corner.)

decoction of lye known as the so-called Schwedentrank; the merciless extortions, the wanton destruction of cattle, grain, crops and domiciles; all these and similar tribulations fell to the lot of Germany during the eventful thirty years from 1618 to 1648.

The armies upon either side were a mere rabble and a gathering of outlaws, robbers and plunderers, who cared more to extort contributions from the defenceless peasant and helpless citizen than to face an armed foe in the cause of the banners under which they fought.

There was but little attempt at uniforming the troops, and with the exception of the French and Hollanders, they were never provided with any distinctive clothing. The great majority of soldiery on both sides could only be told from beggars or strolling vagabonds by the arms they carried. So universal was this the case, that prior to going into battle the various companies would adopt some mark, as a white or red band around the sleeve, or a green sprig in their hats, so that they might distinguish themselves from the foe. Another difference between the armies of the Thirty Years' War and of later wars, was the large number of camp-followers (*Tross*,) and of women (*Tross-weiber*); these two classes in some cases amounted to more than three or four times the number of troops in the field.[129a] No soldier went to the wars in those times unless he took a wife or Tross-woman with him, who not only attended to the cooking, washing and mending for her soldier, but on the march also carried all baggage for which there was no room in the baggage-train.

It was these female camp-followers who were the most dreaded plunderers, and who subjected the helpless matron and maiden of the captured towns and villages to tortures to which death would have been preferable.

Nothing was left undone by these harpies to extract any hidden valuables from the poor victim who

---

[129a] "Geschichte des dreisigjahrigen Krieges," Leipzig 1882. Vol. iii, p. 221.

was handed over into their clutches. A favorite method of torture with them was to remove the flints from the gun-locks, and insert in their place the thumb of the victim, thus improvising one of the most painful instruments of torture.

Another favorite method of these she-monsters was to pierce the tongue and draw a fine horse-hair through it, and then either lead their prisoner thereby or else draw it back and forth. Boring holes in the knee-caps [130] was humane in comparison with other excesses which are upon record, and vouched for in many instances.[131]

At last, after such a terrible scourge of thirty years' duration, the negotiations which commenced in 1643, having for their object a lasting peace, were brought to a close in the year 1648.

The convention which brought this great struggle to a peaceful end, was the outcome of an Imperial diet held at Regensburg, when it was decreed that a meeting of deputies should be convened at Frankfort, in May, 1642. This was, however, delayed until a year later, when the convention adjourned until the following year. It was then resolved that the various peace commissioners should assemble at Münster to treat with the French, and at Osnabruck with the Swedes, and to perfect a protocol which would lead to a lasting peace.

These negotiations extended over several years,

---

[130] "Geschichte des dreisigjahrigen Krieges," Leipzig 1882. Vol. iii, p. 222.
[131] *Ibid*

## Peace of Westphalia.

and it was not until October 24, 1648, that peace resolutions were signed by all parties at Münster. This is what is known in history as the Peace of Westphalia.[132] A large silver medal was struck to commemorate the close of this memorable struggle; a fac-simile of this token showing both obverse and reverse is here reproduced.[132a]

The chief diplomats engaged in this Congress[132b] were Count Troutmannsdorf and Dr. Volmer, upon the part of the Imperialists; d'Avaux and Servien for the French; while count Oxenstierna, son of the great chancellor, and baron Salvius, represented the Swedish interests. In addition to the above, France and Sweden, against the will of the emperor, secured the participation of the estates of the empire in the negotiations.[133]

---

[132] For a full account of these negotiations, see Gindley, dreissigjahrigen Krieges, Leipzig 1882. Vol. iii, pp. 174, *et seq.*

[132a] A specimen is in the collection of Mr. Harry Rodgers of Philadelphia.

[132b] Terburg, the artist, painted a large canvas representing the final scene of this memorable Congress. This painting is now in the Royal gallery at London.

[133] By this peace, the religious and political state of Germany was settled; the sovereignty of the members of the Empire was acknowledged. The changes which had been made for the advantage of the Protestants since the religious peace in 1555, were confirmed by the determination that everything should remain as it had been at the beginning of the [so-called] normal year, 1624. The Calvinists received equal rights with the adherents of the Augsburg Confession or the Lutherans. This peace gave the death-blow to the political unity of Germany. It made the German empire, which was always a most disadvantageous form of government for the people, a disjointed frame without organization or system, a condition from which the nation did not recover until the glorious wars against France in 1870-1.

The final peace, however, was not executed until June 26, 1650, when the historic parchment was signed at Nürnberg,[134] where the occasion was made one of great rejoicing, the chief feature of which was the banquet given in the town hall by the Imperial general, Piccolomini.

The Fatherland, at the conclusion of the peace of Westphalia, was in a pitiable condition. It had suffered an irreparable loss of men and wealth, an unheard-of reduction of population, great increase of poverty, and a retrogression in all ranks of its inhabitants. This was followed by famine and pestilence, and in view of these terrible conditions we may well accept the statement that the population of the Fatherland fell from sixteen millions to four millions, and ended with the almost total annihilation of Germany's wealth and influence.[134a]

Formerly, the German emperor was the acknowledged head of western nations. Now he was shorn of all but the merest shadow of imperial power, and his domain served his enemies and neighboring rulers as a ready object for division and compensation.

In former years the fleet of the German Hansa ruled the ocean, and brought all sorts of foreign products to German ports. Now the glory of com-

---

[134] The rulers of Europe, at the time of the peace of Westphalia: Emperor, Ferdinand IV; Pope, Innocent X; Sultan, Achmet II, son of Ibraim; France, Louis XIV; Spain, Philip IV; England, Charles I; Poland, Casimir; Denmark and Norway, Frederick III; Sweden, Queen Christina; Bohemia, Ferdinand IV; Hungary, Ferdinand IV.

[134a] Sachsse, Ursprung und Wesen des Pietismus Wiesbaden, 1884.

mercial supremacy had been gradually wrested from them, first by the Italians, then by Spain, and later by Holland and England. Thus was Germany cut off from sharing in the riches of the newly discovered regions, or extending her power and influence by colonization.

Nor would it have been possible for Germany under the then existing conditions to aspire to colonial or foreign possessions, for she had by no means been able to maintain her own borders.

Holland and Sweden had long since recognized the importance of foreign extension, which policy resulted in the establishment of West India companies, under whose auspices attempts at settlement were made upon the shores of the Hudson and the Delaware, movements in which we again find German blood prominently represented.

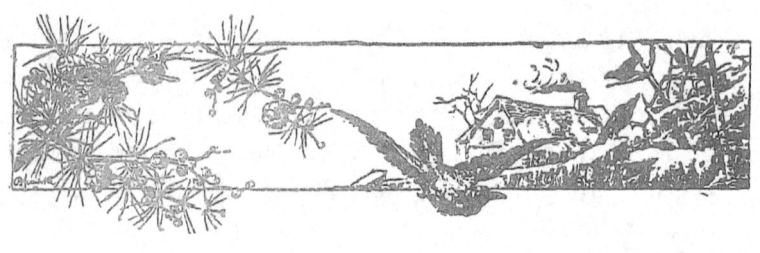

## DUTCH AND SWEDISH ATTEMPTS AT COLONIZATION.

ROYAL ARMS OF HOLLAND.

VARIOUS EXPEDItions were sent out to America from Holland at an early date, and we have vague accounts of attempts at settlements under Cornelius Mey[135] and Verhulst.[135a] It was not, however, until the formation of the Dutch West India Company, an organization projected by Wilhelm Usselinx,[135b] that the first successful effort at colonization was made. This colony was led by Peter Minuet, a German from Wesel,[136] who landed on Manhattan island, May 4, 1626, and there laid the foundation of New Amsterdam, and at the same time that of the Reformed faith in America.

The German soldier, Peter Minuet, was the first governor of the colony of New Netherlands, and acted as ruling elder of the church in the infant settlement.[137] It is a fact worthy of special mention

THE PENNSYLVANIA-GERMAN SOCIETY.

GUSTAVUS ADOLPHUS, KING OF SWEDEN.
(BORN DEC. 9, 1594. DIED NOV. 16, 1632.)

(FROM PAINTING AT HISTORICAL SOCIETY OF PENNSYLVANIA.)

### First Organized Congregation. 133

that the congregation founded on Manhattan island during the reign of Peter Minuet, was the first fully organized Protestant church on the American continent,[128] with a settled pastor, with regularly chosen officers, a list of communicant members, and the stated administration of sacraments.

Treaties were made with the Indians and commercial relations were opened with the Puritans in Massachusetts. The settlers, among whom German blood was largely represented, came here to found

---

[123] The first attempt at Dutch settlement in America was made in the year 1623, under Director Cordelius Mey.

[124] The attempt to found a colony under Verhulst was made in the year 1625.

[125] For the thirty-five different spellings of the name of this pioneer promoter, the reader is referred to Jamison's Willem Usselinx, New York, 1887. Willem Usselinx was born at Antwerp in June, 1567. The exact date of his death is not known, as no record of either his death or burial have thus far been found. He probably died in the year 1647, at the age of eighty years. It does not appear from any of his numerous writings that he ever was married or had any children.

[126] Peter Minnewit (Minuet, Menewe, Meneve, or Menuet) was born at Wesel on the Rhine, of Protestant parentage. Little is known of his early life. There is also a doubt as to the time and place of his death. The most generally accepted account and evidently the true one, is that he was drowned in the harbor of St Christophers, during a a sudden squall upon his return voyage to Sweden. Kapp, in his monograph "Peter Minnewit aus Wesel," München 1866, without citing any authority, states that his death and burial took place at Fort Christina, sometime during the year 1641. The former is however no doubt the true account: certain it is that Minnewit never returned to Europe.

[127] Pastor Michaelius, who served the Reformed Church at New Amsterdam in 1628, mentions the fact in his "Bericht" that the Director Minnewit of Wesel who had acted as Diakon of the Reformed church in his native city, had now assumed the same function in the new church here.

[128] Peter Minuet, by Rev. Cyrus Cort, Dover, Del., p. 23.

homes for themselves and their families; others, again, to establish commercial relations with the old world, and to develop the resources of the new country. All this was in direct contrast to what had thus far been the policy of the heartless and bigoted Spaniard.

As a matter of impartial history;—to the German soldier and adventurer, Peter Minuet, belongs the credit for inaugurating the humane and christian policy of peaceful negotiation and fair dealings with the Indians; a policy for which so much praise has been showered upon William Penn by poet, painter and historian. Yet here, upon the banks of the North river, stood Peter Minuet, a native born German, and director of the Dutch West India Company, bargaining with the Indians for their land (Manhattan island) before he would permit any settlement to be made by his colonists.[139] This scene was enacted just eighteen years before the birth of William Penn and was re-enacted by the same pious adventurer on the banks of the South (Delaware) river some years later, when in the services of Sweden.[140]

Under the administration of Minuet, trade and commerce flourished in the new settlement, immigrants continued to arrive, and the colony from the outset entered upon a career of tranquillity and prosperity.

---

[139] Winsor, Critical History. Vol. iv, p. 398.
[140] This treaty or purchase was concluded from five chiefs of the Minquas, belonging to the great Iroquois race.

Now, what have been the results from this small colony upon the strip of island shore, established there by this German adventurer and christian soldier, Peter Minuet, who was the first European to deal honestly and frankly with the aborigines of the North American colonies, and found a settlement upon principles of humanity and religious tolerance?

The answer is that after the lapse of almost three centuries, the small settlement of Dutch and German nationality has become the Empire state of the American Union, while the little town founded on the extreme end of Manhattan island is now the commercial metropolis of America; and I am proud to say that German influence is to-day even more paramount in commercial, industrial and social circles than it was when the first civil government was established there by the German, Peter Minuet.

After the States-General of Holland, in 1629, introduced the feudal system into their American possessions by what is known as the "Charter for Exemptions and Freedom," Usselinx severed his connection with the Dutch West India Company, and in the next year, 1630, we find him, with his restless activity, seeking to interest Swe-

ROYAL ARMS OF SWEDEN.

den's king in a similar project for colonization in the western world. Two years later, (1632) Peter Minuet also resigned his commission under the Dutch company, and returned to Germany.

As the Swedes at that time were at the height of their power in Germany, it occurred to Usselinx to interest German capital and population in the scheme as well as the Swedish nation. For this purpose he

AUTOGRAPH OF GUSTAVUS ADOLPHUS.

issued a pamphlet called *Mercurius Germaniae*,[141] that is Herald of Germany (or German Mercury) setting forth to the Germans the advantages of his commercial project, and offering them inducements to engage in it, under the amplified charter which was to admit them to participation with the Swedes.

This plan was approved by the king, Gustavus Adolphus, by a patent issued at Nürnberg, dated but a few days prior to the fatal November day when the great Swede fell at Lutzen. An ampflication of this charter had also been prepared, with the king's approval, in favor of the German nation. This document was dated Nürnberg, October 16, 1632, but was left unsigned by the king.

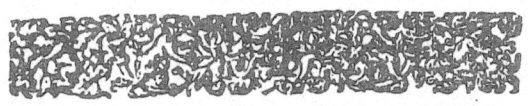

# MERCVRIVS GERMANIÆ.

das ist/

Sonderbahre Anweisung für Teutschlandt:

## Wie beneben dem Allgemeinem
Wesen/ der Kauffhandel vnd Seefahrt/ vnd ins gemein alle Nahrung darinnen sehr zuvermehren vnd zu verbessern : Also das selbige Landt hierdurch zu seinem vorigen Flor vnd Wollstand in kurtzen wiederumb gelangen mögen.

### Erinnerung an den Leser.

Es Jeder Leser/ Ehe vnd zuvor ich zum Hauptwerck schreite/ muß ich den mit wenigen anzeigen: Das G.K.M. von Schweden / Allergroßwürdigsten Ingedencknus/ Kurtz vor dero Seligen Abscheiden/ vnd Insonderheit in Nürnberg/ dieses alhier vorgestellte Werck mit allem Ernst wieder zur Hande genommen / vnd mit Außfertigung deß Privilegii auff die Teutsche Nation vmbgangen : Auch darauff darmal beren nachfolgender discurs entworffen worden. Weil denn nun darneben hero von S. K.M. als noch im Leben vnterschiedlich darinnen gehandelt/ vnd solches auch an jetzo auß grossen Vrsachen nochmaln allenthalben dabey gelassen worden ; Als wollest du derowegen dich dieses nicht irren lassen : Auch darneben dir gantz keine Gedancken machen / als wann durch gedachtes / zwar vns allerseits hoch Trawriges/ Absterben höchstermelter S. K.M. diesem Wercke etwas newe mercklicher difficulteten, so noch nicht in deliberation gezogen/ zugewachsen waren/ davon andersswo mit mehrem.

### Anleitung für Teutschlandt.

Gleicher Gestalt alle Länder vnd Städte durch den Kauffhandel vnd die Seefahrt/ ein grosses Auffnehmen gerahten/ vnnd dadurch bliehen/ wachsen vnd zunehmen / solches hat die Erfahrung zu allen zeiten so vnd Kauffvberflüssig gelehrt vnd bezeuget / daß es vnnötig einigen Geweiß deßfals handels/ vnd anzuführen.   Gleicher massen auch vberflüssig würde fallen / mit vielen Teutschlandes vbeln Zustand. Worten zu erzehlen / wie Teutschlandt durch die Tyranney vnd Reuberey/ wie auch das wilde vnnd vnordentliche wesen deß Keyserischen vnd Spanischen Kriegsvolcks seiner Nahrung vnd Wollstandes beraubet vnd fast gäntzlich ruinieret worden / Inmassen die trawrige Erfahrung solches aller orten vnd enden gnugsam leyder bekant gemachet. So bezeugen gleichfals die täglichen Klagen / das durch die noch immer wehrende beschwerliche Kriegsleufften die Nahrung je mehr vnd mehr in abnehmen gerahten thut/ vnd das hergegen die Beschwerungen vnd Außlagen täglich zunehmen / davon auch noch kein Ende zu spüren oder zu sehen. Darüber den viel Leuthe gäntzlich in solche perturbation vnd Bestürtzung gerahten/ daß sie nicht wissen / was sie ferner gewisses zur hand nehmen sollen/ ihr Hauß nothwendigklich zu vnterhalten/ vnnd dem noch vber haupt schweben dem Vnglück vorzubeugen. Denn sie auch nicht wenig Vrsach haben / weil es der Augenschein gibt/ da ferrin alle Sachen weiter noch eine Zeitlang in einem solchen Zustand wie bißher / verbleiben solten / das noch endtlich viel Leuthe dabey in das eussserste Armuht vnd Elend gerahten vnd verfallen würden.

Welches alles dieweil es gnugsam bekandt ist/ so erfordert ja die höchste Noth/ das/ dieweil Friede vnd Ruhe in allen Stänten so bald well noch nicht zu hoffen/ man auff andere Mittel / wegen Vnd damit dero vbeln Zudencke vnd trachte/ dadurch fernerem Vnheil vnd Verderb vorgebawet/ Teutschland in seinen vorigen stand höchste Wollstand

A

The patent, however, was signed at Heilbronn, April 10, 1633, by the Swedish chancellor, Axel Oxenstjerna[142] who, though a Swede by birth, was a German by adoption and education. In the following May the chancellor, while still at Heilbronn, issued a commission which seems to have been drawn up for the king's signature, empowering Usselinx as chief director of the new South Company to proceed with its immediate organization.

Usselinx, having obtained his enlarged grant, at once issued a German prospectus of 127 pages folio, under the title *Argonautica Gustaviana*.[143] The first item in the contents of the book is a proclamation, or patent by Oxenstjerna, dated Frankfort, June 26, 1633, giving notice of the renewal of the charter, with amplifications and the reappointment of Usselinx, and charging all to assist in so good a work.[144] Meetings were held in different cities[145] during the next twelve months to organ-

SEAL AND AUTOGRAPH OF OXENSTIERNA.

---

[141] "*Mercurius Germaniae*. that is. Special Exposition for Germany." See Jamison, Willem Usselinx, p. 312.

[142] *Ibid*, 317.

[143] This is supposed to be the earliest German book or pamphlet on Emigration. For the bibliography of the Argonautica, see *Ibid*, Appendix No. 26.

[144] *Ibid*, 319.

ARGONAVTICA GVSTAVIANA;
Das ist:
Nothwendige NachRicht
# Von der Newen Seefahrt vnd
Kauffhandlung;

So von dem Weilandt Allerdurchleuchtigsten / Großmächtigsten vnd Siegreichesten Fürsten vnnd Herrn / Herrn GVSTAVO ADOLPHO MAGNO, der Schweden / Gothen vnd Wenden König / Großfürsten in Finnlandt / Hertzogen zu Ehesten vnd Carelen / Herrn zu Ingermanlandt/ic. Allerglorwürdigsten Seeligsten Andenckens/ durch anrichtung einer

## GeneralHandel-COMPAGNIE,
Societet oder Gesellschafft/

In dero Reich vnd Landen / zu derselben sonderbahrem Auffnehmen vnd Flor/auß hohem Verstandt vnd Rath/ vor wenig Jahren zu stifften angefangen:

Anietzo aber der Teutschen Evangelischen Nation / insonderheit den jenigen welche sich in S. K. M. Freundschafft / devotion, oder Verbündnuß begeben / vnd sich dieses grossen Vortheils / bey so stattlicher Gelegenheit/gebrauchen wollen / zu vnermeßlichem Nutz vnd Frommen/auß Königlicher Mildigkeit/zuneigung vnd Gnade/ mitgetheilet worden: vnd mit den förderlichsten/vermittels gnädiger verleihung deß Allerhöchsten/ fortgesetzet vnd völlig zu Werck gerichtet werden soll.

Darauß denn ein jedtweder claren/ gründlichen/ vnd zu seinem Behuff satsamen Bericht vnd Wissenschafft dieses Hochwichtigen Werck's einnehmen / vnd wie dasselbe nicht allein an sich selbst sondern auch dieses orths/ Christlich/ hochrühmlich / Rechtmässig vnd hochnützlich/ auch practicirlich vnd ohne grosse difficulteten sey/ zur gnüge verstehen kan/

Dabey auch zugleich vernünfftig erachten vnnd ermessen mag: Ob seine vnd dem seinigen/ weß Standes oder Conditionis er immer seyn mag/ dieses seines jhme angeworbenen Vortheils / zwischen diesem vnd dem jetzt liebenGott nächst bevorstehenden Newen Jahrs Tage/ durch einschreibung seines Namens vnd einer gewissen Post Geldes/ so sey so viel es wolle/ sich theilhafftig zu machen rathsam vnd thunlich erfunden werden möchte.

Was aber für allerhandt vnterschiedene Schrifften/diese Sache betreffendt/ allhier beysamen vorhanden, solches wird die nachstfolgende Seite zeigen.

1. Regum 9.

Vnd Salomo machte Auch Schiffe zu Ezeon Geber / die bey Eloth ligt am Vfer deß Schilff Meers im Lande der Edomiter : Vnd Hiram der König zu Tyro sandte seine Knechte im Schiff / die gute Schiffleute vnd auff dem Meer erfahren waren/ mit den Knechten Salomo/ vnd kamen gen Ophir / vnd holeten daselbst Vierhundert vnd zwantzig Centner Goldes/ vnd brachtens dem Könige Salomo.

Gedruckt zu Franckfurt am Mayn/bey Caspar Rödeln/
Im Jahr Christi 1633. Mense Junio.
Mit der Cron Schweden Freyheit.

TITLE PAGE OF ARGONAUTICA GUSTAVIANA. ORIGINAL AT HISTORICAL SOCIETY OF PENNSYLVANIA.

ize regular colonies, but just at the time when success seemed assured, the vicissitudes of war, upon the well contested field of Nördlingen, put an end to the undertaking so far as Germany as a nation was concerned.

For a time the project lagged, but it was gradually revived, and in the autumn of 1637 a small expedition, consisting almost entirely of Hollanders and Germans, set out from Gottenberg under Peter Minuet. This little fleet reached the shores of the South (Delaware) river about the middle of March, 1638. Here the scenes enacted twelve years previously on Manhattan island were repeated.[146] On March 29, 1638, a treaty was made with the Indians upon the spot where Wilmington now stands.[147] A colony was started, and the foundation laid of the first regularly organized Lutheran church in America,[148] one of whose chief objects was the christianizing of the Indians, for which the catechism of Luther was translated into the Indian vernacular and printed at an early time long before the century had passed into history.

---

[145] Accounts of some of these meetings held at Frankfort on the Mayn and at Nürnberg. are still in existence.

[146] Peter Minuet Memorial, p. 29.

[147] *Vide* History of New Sweden, by Acrelius; also Ferris, Original Settlements on the Delaware, p. 43.

[148] The colonists at first had their public worship in the fort erected at the landing place. This was the first place dedicated to divine worship in the Christian name on the banks of the Delaware. The first pastor of this congregation was the Rev. Reorus Torkillus, who came out with the expedition, and officiated until his death in 1643.

OXEL OXENSTIERNA.
THE GREAT SWEDISH CHANCELLOR.
(BORN 1583. DIED 1654.)
(FROM ORIGINAL CANVAS AT HISTORICAL SOCIETY OF PENNSYLVANIA.)

# LUTHERI
## Catechismus/

Öfwerſatt
på
American - Virginiſke
Språket.

Stockholm/
Tryckt vthi thet af Kongl. Maytt. privileg.
BURCHARDI Tryckeri/af J. J. Genath/ F.

ANNO M DC XCVI.

TITLE PAGE OF LUTHERAN CATECHISM IN THE INDIAN LANGUAGE. ORIGINAL
IN HISTORICAL SOCIETY OF PENNSYLVANIA.

Peter Minuet, the brave German soldier, never returned from this voyage; but his expedition, small as it was, had sowed the germ of another of the original states of the American Union.

## THE FRENCH WARS OF CONQUEST.

ARMS OF THE CHUR-PFALTZ.

RETURNING ONCE more to Europe, it is found that when eventually France, under the rule of Louis XIV, became the political and intellectual leader of Europe, a policy was inaugurated whereby her borders were extended eastward at Germany's expense. The royal power was asserted by the king, who, aided by Mazarin, used it to further his ambitions and unjust plans of aggrandizement. Thus it became possible for him to maintain his wars of conquest in Holland, devastate Würtemberg and the Palatinate, occupy the city of Strasburg, and eventually detach Alsace and Lorraine.

In this course of rapine and murder upon German soil, the French were neither opposed by the German emperor Leopold, nor by England, which was then rent by internal dissension. In justice to the emperor, it may be said that at that critical period he was even harder pushed in the far east by the Turks, whose triumphant advance was only checked under the walls of Vienna by the bravery of the German-Polish contingent which had been hurriedly gathered.

Sweden had also taken a threatening position in the north, and made attempts to extend her domain southwards from Pomerania:—efforts which were only checked by the glorious victory of the great elector upon the field at Fehrbellin (1675.)

None of these unfortunate warlike movements, however, would have placed the Fatherland in the helpless condition here shown, had it not been for the internal dissensions, political and religious, caused by the quarrel between the emperor and the petty local rulers.

We will now take a glance at the religious situation of Germany at this critical period. After the close of the long war in Europe, Germany, under the continued strain of warlike excitement, was naturally slow in recuperating religiously, financially and intellectually; and in the evangelical sections we again have a long period of unrest, which to some extent spread to the Catholic church, and in which mystical theology played an important part. This condition resulted in what is known as the Pietistical movement in Germany—a striving after some system of personal and practical piety, in opposition to the stiff and dogmatical theology as taught by the clergy after the close of the great war. This movement, in its different phases, spread throughout Europe, and was not confined to the Lutheran church: it extended into the Catholic as well as Calvinistic countries. The Jansenism of Holland, the Quietism of France, the Quakerism of England, all sprang from the same tidal wave of religion as the German Pietism.

The Mennonites, after suffering much persecution, had been recognized as a denomination in the Netherlands, and by the civil authorities were granted equal religious and civil rights with the Reformed: (1626) an act which was afterwards strengthened by a mandate of toleration from the States-General. Under this shelter of religious protection the English Quakers were enabled to introduce their doctrine on the continent at an early day.[149] William Ames went to Holland as early as 1655, and at once entered upon an active missionary career. His ministrations extended from Hamburg in the north to Bohemia in the south, and from the Hague to the kingdom of Poland. In the Palatinate and down the Rhine towards Switzerland, wherever any Mennonites were to be found, there William Ames and his co-laborers, William Caton, Stephen Crisp, George Rolf and others, preached the doctrine of inward light. The missionaries made Amsterdam their headquarters; and two of them—Crisp and Caton—married Dutch women,[150] and thus became citizens of Holland. A number of pam-

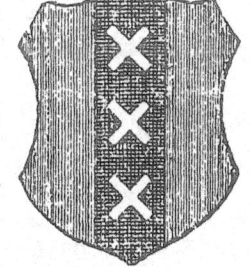

ARMS OF AMSTERDAM.

phlets and counter-pamphlets were among the results of these missionary tours.

The following were the most important of these German missives:

*Ein Klang des Allarms in den Gränzen des Geistlichen Egipten geblasen (welcher in Babilon gehöret werden) and die Inwohner der befleckten und besudelten Wohnungen in der Erde Erschrecken solt, etc. By Stephen Crisp. Amsterdam Gedruckt Anno 1674.*

*Die sache Christi und Seines Volks. With a large preface by B(enjamin) F(urly) 4to 1662. By William Ames.*

*Ein Alarm Geblasen an alle Nationen. 4to 1657.*

*An Euch Alle, etc. 4to 1661. (Relating to the Hat controversy.)*

*Eine Beschirmung der unschuldigen, etc. 4to 1664. (Postscript by Benjamin Furly.)*

*Gewisser Schall der Warheit. 4to. 1665.*

*Ein Wort zur rechter zeit Wider des gewohnlichen Sprichwort, "Ein Geist Bezeuget." 4to. 1675.*

*Die Alte Warheit Erhöhet. (Against the Lutheran Ministerium at Hamburg.) 4to. 1664.*

These last six titles are all by William Caton.

Later on, other English Friends also became prominent in the Low Countries and Germany, some of whom became residents of the continent and permanently identified themselves with the lands of their adoption. Prominent among such was Benja-

---

[149] Penna. Magazine of History and Biography, vol. ii, p. 243.

[150] Stephen Crisp married Gertrude Derricks, a lady of Amsterdam, who was remarkably zealous in the cause of the Quakers.

min Furly,[131] who settled at Rotterdam. Others, again, were merely transient visitors, such as George Fox and William Penn. The latter appears to have made at least three different tours through Holland and Germany, viz:—in 1671 when, with Claus, the Amsterdam bookseller, as a companion and interpreter, he visited Labadie.[132] Secondly, some time in 1674, and thirdly, in the fall of 1677. Several tracts were the result of Penn's second visit to Germany. Two of the most important ones are entitled:

*Send Brieff an die Bürgermeister und Rath der Stadt | Danzig, von Wilhelm Penn, etc. Amsterdam Gedruckt ben Christoff Couraden, Anno 1675.* (Appendix plate I.)

Epistle to the Princess Elisabeth of the Rhine and Countess of Hornes.[132a] London, 1676.

Penn's last visit to the continent was his most important one, when he came to Holland and Germany in company with George Fox and a number of public Friends. Fortunately William Penn's journal[153] of this journey is still in existence.[153a] Nothing is

---

[131] For biographical sketch of Benjamin Furley see the Penna. Magazine of History and Biography, vol. xix, pp. 227, *et seq.* Also, The German Pietists of Provincial Pennsylvania. Philadelphia, 1895 pp. 433, *et seq.*

[132] Croese, Gerhard Croesen's Quaker Historie, Berlin, 1696, pp. 662, *et seq.*

[132a] Penn's original draft of this letter is in the collection of Charles Roberts of Philadelphia.

[153] William Penn's Travels in Holland and Germany, by Oswald Seidensticker. Penna. Mag. vol. ii, pp. 237.

[153a] Penn's MSS Journal of this Journey is now in possession of Charles Roberts of Philadelphia.

known of the itinerary of the previous visits. The general object of this extended tour was to spread the principles and organization of the Society of Friends upon the continent not only among the Mennonites, but now to launch out boldly among the various persons disaffected with the orthodox forms of religion, no matter who they were or where they might be.

*An Account of my JOURNEY into Holland and Germany.*

*WILLIAM PENN.*

*1677.*

TITLE PAGE OF PENN'S MANUSCRIPT JOURNAL. ORIGINAL IN THE COLLECTION OF CHARLES ROBERTS, ESQ., OF PHILADELPHIA.

THE QUAKERS' MEETING HELD AT THE HOUSE OF BENJAMIN FURLY IN THE FALL OF 1677.
(AFTER A PAINTING BY EGBERT HEMSKIRCK THE YOUNGER.)

HEADING OF PENN'S LETTER TO THE COUNTESS OF HORNES, FROM PENN'S MSS. JOURNAL IN POSSESSION OF CHARLES ROBERTS, ESQ., OF PHILADELPHIA.

One of the chief incentives to the movement in Germany were the *Collegia Pietatis* of Spener and his followers,[154] together with the Quietists' movement inaugurated by Molinos, and similar organizations.

It is not within the scope of this paper to follow Fox and Penn in their travels through the Fatherland. Suffice it to say that, although William Penn made two visits to Frankfort to interview Jacob Spener, the great father of Pietism, the latter studiously avoided any meeting or even a semblance of intercourse with the visiting Quakers, carefully guarding himself from any utterances which might be construed into an endorsement of their doctrines; and this in spite of the fact that both Fox and Penn, when in Frankfort,[156] were the guests of Johanna von Merlau, and had preached at her house.

This visit of William Penn to Germany, coached

---

[154] See letter of Penn to the Countess of Hornes. An Account of W. Penn's Travails, etc. Second Impression, London, 1695.

[155] Spener, in his *Freyheit der Glaübigen* (Franckfurt am Mayn, 1691), chapter vii, p. 117, emphatically denies the aspersion made by Dr. Meyer of Hamburg, that nothing was known in Leipzig of the Quakers, until after the formation of the *Collegium Pietatis*. Spener further challenges Dr. Meyer to give the name of a single individual who became convinced of Quakerism through his connection with the *Collegium Pietatis*, or to quote any case where a Quaker had even gained an entrance to the *Collegium*, while he, Spener, was present in Leipzig He further brands as a base calumny the charge accusing him of fraternizing or having any intercourse with the Quaker leaders. In conclusion, Spener states that if any Quakers were to be found in Leipzig they came there independently and of their own accord, and may have been there prior to the formation of his *Collegium Pietatis*.

[156] Penna. Magazine, vol. ii, p. 261.

PHILIP JACOB SPENER.
b. January 13, 1635; d. February 5, 1705.

as he was by Benjamin Furly, brought forth a number of interesting tracts :[156a] four of these being of an hortatory character were written by Penn, and left with Furly for revision and translation, and were afterwards published by him at his own expense.

The titles are:

*Forderung der Christenheit fürs Gericht.* (A call to Christendom, etc.) (*Appendix plate II.*)

"*Eine Freundliche heymsuchung in der Liebe Gottes.*" (A Tender Visitation in the Love of God.) (*Appendix plate III.*)

"*An alle diejenigen so unter den Bekennern der Christenheit,*" etc. (To all Professors of Christianity, etc.)

"*An alle diejenigen welche empfinden,*" etc. (Tender Counsel.)

The above were also published collectively in Dutch under the general title:

"*Het Christenrijk Ten Oordeel Gedagvaart,*" etc. Rotterdam 1678, 4to. (*Appendix plate IV.*)

Two of the above tracts—"A Call to Christendom," and "Tender Counsel," were printed separately at the time in English.

The above tour of William Penn through Germany was purely a religious one; as he himself expresses it, "in the service of the Gospel." It had, however, the effect of bringing him into personal contact with many of the German Mystics and other religious leaders of the period.

---

[156a] Biographical sketch of Benjamin Furly. *Ibid* vol. xix, pp. 277.

Four years later, when the grant from Charles II to Penn was finally consummated, the attention of both Penn and Furly was at once directed to Germany as a field from which to obtain a desirable class of emigrants. Communications were opened forthwith with some of the chief leaders in the Pietistical movement at Frankfort, and the religious Separatists at Krisheim and the vicinity,—men and women with whom Penn had become acquainted during his visits to Germany. These efforts upon the part of Benjamin Furly resulted in the formation of two companies. The one at Frankfort was a regularly organized corporation, known as the "Frankfort Company," which according to Pastorius consisted of the following persons:[157] Jacob Van de Walle, Doctor Johann Jacob Schutz, and Daniel Behagel, Handelsmann,[157a] of Frankfort; Doctor Gerhard von Mastrich, of Duisburg; Doctor Thomas von Wylich and Herr Johann Lebrunn, of Wesel; Benjamin Furly, of Rotterdam; and Mr. Philip Fort, of London. According to other accounts the original company consisted of Jacob Van de Walle, Caspar Merian, Doctor Johann Jacob Schutz, Johann Wilhelm Uberfeldt, George Strauss, Daniel Behagel, Johann

AUTOGRAPH OF BENJAMIN FURLY.

---

[157] Umstandige Geographische Beschreibung Der zu allerletzt erfundenen Provintz Pennsylvanae, etc. F. D. Pastorius, Franckfurt und Leipzig, 1700, p 35.
[157a] Merchant.

WILLIAM PENN.
b. 1644; d. 1718.

Laurentz and Abraham Hasevoet. This company secured 15,000 acres of land in the new colony, and sent out Francis Daniel Pastorius as their agent and attorney.

The other company known as the Crefeld colony, was organized upon a different basis, the members purchasing their land in an individual, and not in a corporate capacity.[158]

SEAL OF WILLIAM PENN.

The members composing this company were mostly from Krisheim and Crefeld, and had secured the land for the purpose of settling in the new Province.

It was this latter contingent that crossed the ocean in the Concord a few months later, and landed at Philadelphia on the sixth of October, 1683. An event which William Penn made the subject of a special letter to England, dated November 10, 1683, wherein he rejoices at the continued good fortune of the Province, and the arrival of so many people from Crefeld and the neighboring places in the land of "Meurs."[159]

To properly place the advantages of Pennsylvania before the various races of German people, and thus induce a large emigration, a number of tracts or

---

[158] For the amount of land held by these first purchasers, see Pennypacker, Settlement of Germantown, Phila., 1883, p. 31.

pamphlets, descriptive and otherwise, were issued by
Penn, Furly and others, in
both high and low German, for the purpose of
giving the requisite information to prospective settlers. Some of these
brochures were translations
of the prospectus issued
by Penn in England;
others again were written
with special reference to
the requirements of the
Germans.

Arms of Penn.

As these tracts are all excessively scarce, and as
they contain the most reliable information we have
regarding the planting of the colony, a list of the
series so far as known is here enumerated, with
notes as to where the originals are to be found, and is
further supplemented by an Appendix at the close of

---

[159] Meurs, (Mörs) a former German Principality, bounded by the
Bishopric of Cologne, and the principalities of Cleve, Berg and Geldern,
and the Rhine. It contained about 28000 inhabitants, who were mainly
of the Protestant faith, chiefly Reformed. During the Napoleonic wars
it was ceded by treaty to France in 1801, but was recovered by Prussia
at the treaty of Paris in 1814. It is now a part of the Department of
Düsseldorf. The former capital, Meurs, is a town of Rhenish Prussia,
17 miles N.N.E. of Düsseldorf, on the Eider. It has Lutheran and
Roman Catholic churches, a normal school, and a town-hall in front of
which are the sculptured lions found on the site of the Asciburgum of
Tacitus. Under the French, Meurs was the capital of the department of
Roer.

this paper showing fac-similes of the various title pages.

First upon the list is the Royal Proclamation, or the King's declaration of his grant to William Penn. It was issued under date of April 2, 1681, and is addressed:

" To the Inhabitants and Planters of the Province of Pennsylvania : "

Next we have Penn's :

"Certain Conditions or Concessions Agreed upon by William Penn, Proprietary and Governor of the Province of Pennsylvania, and those who are the Adventurers and Purchasers in the Same Province, the Eleventh of July, One Thousand Six Hundred and Eighty-one."

No pamphlet copy of this tract is known.

Almost immediately after the grant of the Province was confirmed to William Penn, he published an account of it from the best information he then had. It is printed in a folio pamphlet of ten pages, and is entitled :

Some | account | of the | Province | of | Pennsilvania | in | America ; | Lately Granted under the Great Seal | of | England | to | William Penn, &c. | [160] London: Printed, and Sold by Benjamin Clark | Bookseller in George-Yard Lombard-street, 1681 | (*Appendix plate V.*)

---

[160] Copies of this tract, (folio 11¼ x 7¼ inches,) are to be found at the Historical Society of Pennsylvania, The Carter Brown Library and Harvard College Library. The chief portions of the tract are reprinted

This tract was translated into both high and low German.

Eine | Nachricht | wegen der Landschaft | Pennsilvania | in | America : | Welche | Jüngstens unter dem Grossen Siegel | Engelland | an | William Penn, &c | [161] In Amsterdam gedruckt bey Christoff Cunraden. | Im Jahr 1681. | (Appendix plate VI.)
This is the earliest German account of Pennsylvania. Two years later (1683) it was reprinted at Leipzig. It also formed a part of the *Diarium Europaeum.*

Een kort Bericht | Van de Provintie ofte Landschap | Penn-sylvania | genaemt, leggende in | America; | Nu onlangs onder het groote Zegel van Engeland | gegeven aan | William Penn, &c. | [162] Tot Rotterdam. | Gedrukt by Pieter van Wynbrugge, Bock-Drukker in de | Leeuwestraat, in de Wereld Vol-Druk. Anno 1681. | (Appendix plate VII.)
By referring to the fac-similes of the two latter titles in the Appendix, it will be found that Furly, to further strengthen Penn's claims to German recognition and to stimulate emigration, had added a

---

in Hazard's Annals of Pennsylvania. Also in Hazard's Register, vol. i, p. 305. For notice of, see Penna. Mag. of History, vol. iv, p. 187.

[161] Copies are at the Historical Society of Pennsylvania, Carter Brown Library and in Loganian Library, Philadelphia. See also Penna. Mag. of History, vol. xix, p. 287, and The German Pietists of Provincial Pennsylvania, Phila. 1895, p. 446.

[162] A copy of the Dutch Translation is in the Carter Brown Library. Also in the Archiv der Gemeentee, Rotterdam. See Penna. Mag. of History, vol. xix, p. 288. Also, German Pietists of Pennsylvania, p. 447.

translation of Penn's "Liberty of Conscience" (*Appendix plate VIII*) to the original "Some Account" which gave a mere description of his newly acquired Province.

The two following titles were published during the same year (1681,) and although not at the instance of either Penn or Furly, yet they did much to bring the Province to the notice of the Huguenot refugees, and to the Germans of the middle and educated classes, especially such as lived in the valley of the Rhine.

*Petri du Val,—Geographiae Universalis. Das ist Der allgemeinen Erd Beschreibung. Darinnen die Drey Theil der welt nemlich America, Africa und Asia, etc. . . Nürnberg. In verleg. Johann Hoffman's Buch und Künsthandlers. Gedruckt daselbst bey Christian Siegmund Froberg. M.DC.LXXXI*[163] (*Appendix plate IX.*)

"*Recit des l' estat present des celebres colonies de la Virgine, de Marie-Land, de la Caroline, du noveau Duche' d' York, de Pennsylvania, et de la Nouvelle Angleterre, situees dan s l' Amerique Septentrionale, etc. A Rotterdam, Chez Reinier Leers. M.DC.LX-XXI. 4to. 43pp. with three folding plates.*[164] (*Appendix plate X.*)

Resuming the publications of Penn and Furly, we next have the important pamphlet entitled:

---

[163] Original in Carter Brown Library. Catalogue vol. ii, Number 1217.
[164] *Ibid.*

The | Articles | Settlement and Offices | Of the free | Society | of | Traders | in | Pennsilvania: | Agreed upon by divers | Merchants | And others for the better | Improvement and Government | of | Trade | in that | Province[165] | London, | Printed for *Benjamin Clark* in *George-Yard* in *Lombard-street* | Printer to the Society of *Pennsilvania*, MDCLX-XXII | (*Appendix plate XI.*)

These articles were agreed to March 25, 1682, and as stated by Hazard [165a] were published in folio upon the day following.

The Charter granted by Penn to the "Free Society of Traders in Pennsylvania" was recorded at Doylestown among the records of Bucks County. It was first printed in Hazard's Annals of Pennsylvania.[165a] Philadelphia, 1850, pp. 541-550.

The above tract was quickly followed by the publication of Penn's Frame of Government:

The Frame of the | Government | of the | Province of Pennsilvania | in | America | Together with certain | Laws | Agreed upon in England | By the | Governour | and | Divers free-men of the aforesaid ¦ Province | To be further Explained and Confirmed there by the first | *Provincial Council* and *General Assembly* that shall | be held, if they see meet | Printed in the year MDCLXXXII | (*Appendix plate XII*)[166]

---

[165] Original in the Historical Society of Pennsylvania. It is a small folio of sixteen pages. The outside measurement of the ruling which surrounds the title page is 10¼ x 6 in. Tract was republished in full in the Penna. Mag. of History and Biography, vol. v., pp. 37-50.

Penn's own copy with his book-plate is in the collection of the Historical Society of Pennsylvania. It is from this copy that the fac-simile (*plate XII*) is made.

Shortly after the publication of the two latter pamphlets, there was issued a small folio of three and a half pages, two columns to a page, the object of which was to furnish information for prospective settlers, and set forth the advantages of Penn's Province. The heading of the first page reads:

" Information and Direction | to | Such Persons as are inclined | to | America, | More | Especially Those related to the Province | of Pennsylvania.[167] | (*Appendix plate XIII.*)

It then goes on to state:

"That the Value and Improvement of *Estates* in our Parts of *America*, may yet appear with further clearness and Assurance to Enquirers, I propose to speak my own Knowledge, and the Observation of others, as particularly as I can; which I shall comprise under these Heads:"

I. The Advance that is upon Money and Goods.

II. The advance that is upon Labour, be it of Handicrafts or others.

III. The Advance that is upon Land.

IV. The Charge of Transporting a Family, and Fitting a Plantation.

---

[166a] Annals of Pennsylvania, Phila., 1850.

[167] Copies of this pamphlet are also to be found in the Carter Brown Library, of Providence, R. I., and the Harvard College Library.

V. The way the Poorer sort may be Transported, and Seated, with Advantage to the Rich that help them.

VI. The easier and better provision that is to be made there for Posterity, especially by those that are not of great Substance.

VII. What Utensils and Goods are fitting to carry for Use or Profit."

The authorship of this tract has been attributed to Penn; and while there is nothing to prove the assertion, it was undoubtedly prepared under his direction.

Both German and Dutch translations of this pamphlet were made, the conditions being somewhat modified so as to adapt themselves to the requirements of the Germans and Dutch. No German copy of this rare pamphlet is known. A Dutch copy, lacking the last pages and imprint, was found among the Penn papers in the Historical Society's collection; it is endorsed " Dutch information over Pennsylv." Like the English original it merely starts with a heading:

*Nader Informatie of Onderrechtinge voor de gene die|genegen zijn om na America te gaan, en|wel voornamentlijk voor die geene die in de Provin|tie van Pensylvania geintresseert zijn.* (*Appendix plate XIV.*)

A later Dutch edition, with a somewhat different heading was issued in 1686.[168]

---

[167] Copy in Collection of Historical Societs of Penna. It was reprinted in the Penna. Mag. of History and Biography, vol. iv., p. 330. A Second Edition was printed in Amsterdam, 1686.

Before the end of the year, Penn published another tract, for the purpose of inducing emigration to Pennsylvania; the title was:

A brief Account of the | Province of Pennsylvania, | Lately Granted by the | King | Under the Great | Seal of England, | to | William Penn | and his | Heirs and Assigns,[169] | London. (*Appendix plate XVI.*)

This was quickly translated and published by Furly in several continental languages, Dutch, French[170] and German. The heading of the latter reads:

*Kurtz Nachricht Von der Americanischen Landschafft Pennsylvania.*[171] (*Appendix plate XVI.*)

There was still another work issued in 1682, having for its express object the furthering of emigration to America:

Plantation Work | the | Work | of this | Generation. | Written in True-Love. | To all such as are weightily inclined | to Transplant themselves and Fami | lies to any of the English Plantati | ons in | America | The | most material Doubts and Objections against it | being removed, they may more cheerfully pro | ceed to the Glory and Renown of the God of | the whole Earth, who in all Undertakings is to | be looked unto, Praised and Feared for Ever.[172]|London, 1682. (*Appendix plate XV.*)

---

[168] Copy in Carter Brown Library.
[169] Copies of this tract are in the Collection of the Historical Society of Penna., and the library of Harvard College.

This work contains several abstracts of letters from Pennsylvania dated December 1681; it does not appear to have been translated.

The flood of pamphlets, so freely scattered over northern Germany by Furly in the interests of Penn, attracted the attention of no less a personage than Frederick William, elector of Brandenburg, usually styled "the Great Elector," and the founder of the present Prussian monarchy. The battle of Fehrbellin had been fought and won, completely routing the Swedes. By the subsequent treaty with both Sweden and France, he received large sums of money and came into possession of a small fleet. The elector now devoted himself to establish institutions of learning and to extend the influence of his dominions.

The first duty assigned to his small navy was to enter upon an expedition in the interest of a German colonization scheme, which he had proposed as an offset to the threatened exodus of German yeomanry to the British possessions in America.

For this purpose two of the staunchest vessels of the new navy, the frigates "Chur-printz" and "Morian," under the command of Otto Friedrich von der Gröben, were sent upon a voyage of discovery, to

---

[170] The writer has seen a copy of the French edition, but has never met with a copy of the Dutch tract.

[171] The only known copy is in the collection of the Historical Society of Pennsylvania.

[172] Copies of Plantation work are at the Penna. Historical Society, the Carter Brown Library, and Friends Library, Philadelphia.

Flag-ship of the German Squadron in the Harbor of Gluckstat, May, 1682. Fac-simile of a Sketch in V. Groben's Report.

settle upon the best site for a German colony under the standard of the Great Elector and thereby extend his domain beyond the sea.

The instructions of von der Gröben were to visit the west coast of Africa, as well as the east coast of North America, returning by way of Ireland, and to report upon such location as would be best suited for a German colony.

The little fleet weighed anchor at Hamburg on May 16, 1682, stopping at Glückstadt and Kockshaven for supplies and additional soldiery. The expedition, after many vicissitudes incident to the elements, eventually reached the coast of Africa; landings were made at different points, and barter with the natives instituted; a landing was made on the Gold Coast, a fortification was built, and upon January 1, 1683, official possession was taken with considerable ceremony. The great standard of Brandenburg was unfurled amidst the firing of cannon and the music of kettle-drums and shawms (Pauken und Schallmeyen.) In honor of the Great Elector the post or station was named *Der Grosse Friedrichs-Berg*. This occupation led to an embroglio with the Hollanders, who claimed the territory. The Germans, however, maintained possession.

While von der Gröben was engaged in the establishment and fortification of his colony, the settlers were stricken with the fevers incident to that coast and von der Gröben himself was seriously ill on the frigate *Morian*. While the expedition was in this sad plight, the commander of the Chur-Printz suddenly left with his vessel, sailed along the coast and engaged in slave-trade.[173]

---

[173] Reise-Beschreibung, Des Brandenburgischen Adelichen Pilgers. Otto Friedrich von der Gröben. Marienwerder, Gedruckt durch Simon Reinegern. Anno 1694. (A copy of this book is in library of the writer.)

Von der Gröben, upon his recovery, in pursuance of his original instructions, left the African coast and sailed for America by way of the Flemish Islands (Azores.) It does not appear from his published report that he made any attempts either to land or colonize in the western hemisphere. He appears to have sailed as far north as Newfoundland, where he traded for codfish. Thence, he headed eastward, he skirted the coast of Ireland, and arrived at the mouth of the Elbe in October, 1683, the voyage having lasted eighteen months.

The German settlement thus established upon the coast of Africa was subsequently reinforced, and gradually spread along the coast, so that in the year 1687, the flag of Brandenburg waved over four different settlements and fortified trading-stations in that region. The insalubrity of the climate, and the failure of any requisite pecuniary return, caused these settlements to be abandoned after the death of the Great Elector, which occurred on April 29, 1688.

In looking over this almost forgotten episode in the history of attempted German colonization, one is naturally startled at the thought of how far-reaching the results might have been, if the German commander had sailed direct to the American coast and obtained a foothold here, instead of wasting his men and resources in the vain attempts upon the Gold coast.

Had he unfurled the standard of the Great Elector upon these shores, where the climate would have been congenial, and had the wise plans of Frederick

William been carried out, either by treaty or otherwise, with such power as claimed sovereignty over American soil, the thousands of German yeomen who left the Fatherland during the next three decades to be scattered over these shores, and in a great measure developed the British colonies in America, might have been concentrated within a single province under the German standard, which undoubtedly would have proven a nucleus for a German empire in the western world.

Here arise possibilities for thought almost too great for contemplation. However, as a matter of fact, the failure of the elector's plans for German colonization must be laid to the avarice or incapacity of those into whose hands was placed the execution of his plans, and not to the wise intentions of the great ruler whose living monument is virtually the great German empire of the present day.

ARMS OF BRANDENBURG.

## GERMAN EMIGRATION TO AMERICA.

ARMS OF WÜRTEMBERG.

WE now come to the immediate cause of the great emigration to America, the emigration of what was left of the German population within the Palatinate and the Duchy of Würtemberg after the French invasions.

The edict of Nantes, it will be remembered, was revoked on October 18, 1685, by which the exercise of the Reformed religion in France was forbidden, children were to be educated in the Catholic faith, and all emigration was prohibited.

In spite of the latter command, however, many of the persecuted Huguenots flocked across the borders and accepted the shelter offered them by the Palatine Elector.[174] This induced the notorious Madame de Maintenon, a narrow minded bigot, to induce the king utterly to devastate the Palatinate, and peremptory orders were given through Louvois that the

Palatinate should be destroyed. In pursuance of this command 100,000 French soldiers were despatched by Louis XIV, to do the work. How well this horde of murderers did his bidding is a matter of history. Even to the present day, after the lapse of two centuries, the line of march may be traced from the Drachenfels to Heidelberg. Crumbling walls, ruined battlements and blown-up towers, still remain as mementoes of French vandalism.

The league of Augsburg was formed, but failed to save the fated Fatherland from French pillage and rapine. Hardly had the smoke from the blazing embers died away from one invasion, and the fields and vineyards once more begun to show signs of peaceful thrift, than another invasion followed and swept with a frightful desolation over the doomed valley of the Rhine.

This devastation extended into the Duchy of Würtemberg, and it may be said that in the years 1688-9 the whole of southern Germany was overrun by the French and completely paralyzed with the fear of the hireling murderers. The tale of this devastation of the fertile *Schwabenland* has been ably set forth by one of Würtemberg's most learned historians, upon the occasion of the bi-centennial anniversary.[175]

The chief factors in this blot upon civilization were

---

[174] Penna. Mag. of History and Biog. vol. vi, p. 318.
[175] *Württemberg und die Franzosen im Jahr 1688, von Theodor Schott, Stuttgart, 1888.*

The Burgomaster's Wife at Schorndorf, before the Council.
After an oil painting by Haberlin, at Stuttgart.

the French ambassador at the court of Würtemberg, D'Invigney, and Melac, the commander of the military forces ; and in so great detestation is the name of the latter held, that even to the present day, "Melac" is one of the favorite names for Suabian dogs.

The story of how this unaccountable fear of the French was eventually overcome, and the period of German inactivity terminated, is a well-known episode in German history. Allusion is here made to the Burgomaster's wife at Schorndorff, Anna Barbara Walch, a small courageous woman, who, when she received an intimation that the Stadt-rath or council were considering a demand of surrender by the French, went to the town-hall, called her husband out and threatened him with death if he dared to vote for surrender. She then assembled a number of equally brave women, who armed themselves with forks, broom-handles, and other domestic weapons, surrounded the town-hall, and by main force prevented the council from surrendering the town.

The denouement of this uprising is also well known. Schorndorff was saved, the French were defeated, and eventually driven out of Würtemberg.

This incident is purposely introduced here, as there were many Frankish and Palatinate women of equal courage who came here to Pennsylvania and helped to make this Commonwealth : women whose descendants are now members of our society : men who have lost none of the courage, bravery or patriotism imparted to them by their German maternal ancestors.

Without going into further particulars regarding

the succeeding conflicts that rent the Fatherland, suffice it to say that it was this ruthless desolation of the valley of the Rhine, more than any other cause, that started the great and steady stream of German blood, muscle and brains, to Pennsylvania's sylvan shores.

At this period of the Fatherland's helplessness and desolation, the darkest days of Germany's humiliation, messengers were again sent forth to the various towns and in the valley of the Rhine, bearing the news that the scheme of William Penn, the Quaker, was a successful one, and that the Province or the Quaker-valley (*Quackerthal*) was open to all persons who refused to conform to the requirements of the orthodox religion as by law established.[176]

The chief promoter of this scheme for German emigration was the same Benjamin Furly, the English Quaker and merchant at Rotterdam, whose acquaintance we have previously made as the companion and interpreter of William Penn during the latter's visit to Germany and Holland in 1677.

It is at this point that a special tribute is due to Benjamin Furly for his efforts to throw safeguards around the German emigrant who was not conversant with either English language, customs or laws.

William Penn, in drafting the fundamental laws

---

[176] Spener, in his *Freyheit der Gläubigen*, Franckfurth-am-Mayn, 1691, enumerates the following sects of Separatists (Chap. viii, p. 118) Weigelians, the Rosicrucians, Arminians, different kinds of Syncretists, Osianderians, those who could not bear religious vows; Pseudo Philosophers, Anti-Scripturalists, Latitudinarians, Chiliasts and Böhmists.

of his Province, submitted the various drafts to Benjamin Furly and possibly to others. Furly not only compared the different "Frames of Government," "Fundamentall Constitutions," and laws prepared for the Province; but offered substitutes and suggestions to the Proprietor, containing provisions for the protection of such as were about to transport themselves and their families to Pennsylvania at the latter's solicitation. He even criticized the Proprietor, where, in the proposed laws, changes were made which did not meet with his approval. Two of these documents, in Furly's handwriting, have been found among the Penn papers, now in the collection of the Historical Society of Pennsylvania. One is endorsed:

"For the Security of Forreigners who may incline to purchase Land in Pennsylvania, but may dy before they themselvs come to their inhabit."

This paper was published in full, with an introduction, by Frederick D. Stone Litt. D., to the Sketch of Benjamin Furly by the writer, in the Penna. Magazine of History and Biography, October, 1895.[177] The other paper is a comment on "The Fundamentall Constitutions." The manuscript of which was found among the "Penn Papers" in possession of the Historical Society of Pennsylvania, and published by the Society in October, 1896.[178]

---

[177] Penna. Mag. of Hist. and Biog. vol. xix, p. 295.

[178] "The Fundamentall Constitutions of Pennsilvania. *Ibid* vol. xx, p. 283, *et seq.*

These papers show the intimate concern Furly felt in the laws and government of the new province and the welfare of the German settlers. The former document is a valuable one to every student interested in the development of our country, but especially for Pennsylvania Germans, as it shows how earnestly Furly stood up for their ancestors' personal rights and estate.[179]

Then again, his suggestions and advice to Penn as to the course to pursue in regard to a possible attempt to introduce negro slavery into the Province, is of great interest, as the first public protest against this evil in America was made at Germantown in 1688 by some of the German pioneers who came to Pennsylvania under his auspices and bounty.

FAC-SIMILE OF ANTI-SLAVERY CLAUSE IN FURLY'S SUGGESTIONS TO PENN.

---

[179] See Articles I and II. *Ibid* vol. xix, p 297.

## LITERATURE USED TO INDUCE GERMAN EMIGRATION.

The various pamphlets and tracts issued by Penn and Furly, were:

"A | Letter | from | William Penn | Proprietary and Governour of | Pennsylvania | In America, | to the | Committee | of the | Free Society of Traders | of that Province, residing in London, | etc.[180] Printed and Sold by Andrew Sowle, at the Crooked-Billet in Holloway-Lane in Shoreditch, and at several Stationers in London, 1683." (*Appendix plate XIX.*)

This pamphlet was quickly translated and issued in low Dutch, German and French:

"*Missive | van | William Penn, | Eygenaar en Gouverneur van | Pennsylvania, | in America. | Geschreven aan de Commissarissen van de Vrye Socie | teyt der Handelaars, op de Provintie, | binnen London resideerende. | etc.*[181] Amsterdam Gedrukt voor Jacob Claus, Boekverkooper in de Prince-straat, *1684*. (*Appendix plate XX.*)

*Beschreibung | Der in America neu-erfundenen | Provintz | Pensylvanien. | Derer Inwohner, Gesetz, Arth, Sit | ten und Gebrach: | Auch samtlicher Reviren des Landes | Sonderlich der Haupt-Stadt | Phila-delphia | Alles glaubwurdigst | Auss des Governeurs darinnen erstatteten | Nachricht. | In Verlegung bey Henrich Heuss an der Banco | im Jahr 1684.*[182] (*Appendix plate XXI.*)

*Recueil | de | Diverses | pieces | Concernant | la | Pensylvanie. | A la Haye, | Chez Abraham Troyel, | Marchand Libraire, dans la Grand Sale | de la Cour, M.DC. LXXXIV.*[183] (*Appendix plate XXII.*)

The above three tracts in addition to Penn's letter to the "Free Society of Traders," contained Holme's description of Philadelphia, and Thomas Paskel's letter dated February 10, 1683, u. s.

---

[180] Originals in Historical Society of Penna., New York Historical Society, and Philadelphia Library. Six different editions were issued during the year. This tract contains the first printed account of Philadelphia by the founder of the Colony.

[181] Copies of this tract are in Collection of Hist. Soc. of Penna., and Carter Brown Library of Providence. This tract is also exceedingly rare, and contains a letter from Thomas Paschal, dated Philadelphia Feb'y 10, 1683. The first dated from that locality. Two editions were printed in low Dutch, with some variation in the title page; it contains the imprint *Den Tweeden Druk* 1684. It also contains a plan of the City.

[182] One of the scarcest Pennsylvania pamphlets. The only known copy is in the Carter Brown Collection of Providence from which the fac-simile in Appendix is made.

[183] Copies of this excessively rare volume are in the Carter Brown Library and the Library of a Philadelphia collector. The copy in the British Museum lacks the title page  The important parts of this book "collection of various pieces concerning Pennsylvania" were translated by Hon. Sam'l W. Pennypacker and printed in the Penna. Mag., of Biography and History, vol. vi, pp. 311-328.

A later French edition, printed at Amsterdam, 1688, also contains Penn's "Further Account" of 1685, Turner's Letter, and :—

"Explanations of Mr. Furly to purchasers and renters upon certain articles concerning the establishment of Pennsylvania. Rotterdam, 1684.[184] (*Appendix plate XXIII.*)

The above issues offer an interesting study, as they were supplemented to at this time by some accounts written by actual residents in Pennsylvania, and thereby went far to stimulate the German emigration. The earliest of these pamphlets appears to have been a single sheet or two leaves quarto; it bore the following title:

*Twee Missiven geschreven uyt Pennsilvania a' Ene door een Hollander woonachtig in Philadelfia, d' Ander door Switzer, woonachtig in German Town, Dat is Hoogduytse Stadt. Van den 16, Maert, 1684. Nieuwen Stijl. Tot Rotterdam, Anno 1684.* 2 leaves small 4to.[185]

This tract is an exceedingly scarce one. The copy examined by the writer was in the Archive of the City of Rotterdam.

---

[184] No English edition of Furly's "Explanations" is known to the writer. A translation into English from the French Edition, 1684, by Hon. Sam'l W. Pennypacker will be found in Penna. Mag. Biography and History, vol. vi, p. 319, *et seq.*

[185] Copy in Archief der Gemeente Rotterdam, Holland. There is also a copy in the Library of Congress (which unfortunately was not available at the time our appendix was prepared). This interesting pamphlet was translated by Hon. S. W. Pennypacker. See "Hendrick Pennebecker, Surveyor of Lands for the Penns," by Hon. S. W. Pennypacker, privately printed, Philadelphia, 1894. Chapter iii, pp. 27-39.

The next important work upon the list is Thomas Budd's "Good Order Established;" this was printed by Bradford in Philadelphia :[186]

"Good Order Established | in | Pennsilvania & New Jersey | in America, | Being a true account of the Country ; | With its Produce and Commodities there made, etc. . . By Thomas Budd. Printed in the year 1685." (*Appendix plate XXIV.*)

Another account, a more pretentious one, was by Cornelis Bom, a Dutch baker, who came to Philadelphia at an early date and here plied his trade. This book was published at Rotterdam, 1685, by Pieter van Wijnbrugge, a Dutch Quaker and Publisher:[187]

*Missive van | Cornelis Bom, | Geschreven uit de Stadt | Philadelphia, | In de Provintie van | Pennsylvania, | Leggende op d' Oostzyde vande | Zuyd Revier van Nieuw Nederland. | Verhalende de groote voortgank | van de selve Provintie, | Waer by komt | De Getuygenis van | Jacob Telner | van Amsterdam.* | (*Appendix plate XXV.*)

These publications were followed by :

A Further Account of the Province | of Pennsylvania, and its Improvements. | For the Satisfaction of those that are Adventurers, and | Inclined to be so.[188] (*Appendix plate XXVI.*)

This Account was signed "William Penn" and dated at the end—"Worminghurst Place" 12, of

---

[186] Original in Historical Society of Penna.
[187] Originals are in collection of Hist. Soc. of Penna., and in the archives of the Moravian Church at Bethlehem, Penna.
[188] Copy in Hist. Soc. of Penna.

the 10th month, 1685. Two editions of it are known to have been published.

A Dutch translation was published early in the following year, this tract is exceedingly rare:

*Tweede | Bericht ofte Relaas | Van | William Penn, | Eygenaar en Gouverneur van de Provintie van | Pennsylvania, | In America, etc. Amsterdam by Jacob Claus, Boekverkoper in de Prince-straat.*[189] (*Appendix plate XXVII.*)

It is not to be assumed that the efforts upon the part of Penn and Furly, followed by the willing response of so many German yeomen, were left unnoticed by the authorities, both religious and secular, of the German provinces affected, which were already so depleted by the successive wars.

Numerous edicts were issued by the ruling Princes, in such a manner that they included Pietist as well as Quaker within their scope. The most important anathemas at this period are the following:[190]

Sr. Chür Furstl. Durchl. zu Sachsen, Joh. Georg des Dritten, Befehl wider die neuerlich angestellten *Conventicula* oder *Privat* Zusammenkünffte. *Publiciret* den 25, Martii 1690.

Der Durchlauchtigsten Fürsten und Herren, Herr Rudolph Augustus, und Herr Anthon Ulrichs, Gebrüdere, Hertzogen zu Braunschweig und Lüneburg, *Edict* und Verordnung, wegen der hin und wieder sich erreigenden Neuerungen und *Sectareyen. Publiciret* den 2, Martii, Anno 1692.

---

[1-9] The only known originals are in the Carter Brown Library of Providence and collection of Historical Society of Penna.

[190] Copies of the following Edicts, are in the collection of the Historical Society of Penna., and in the Library of the writer.

Ihrer Küniglichen Majestät in Schweden *Caroli*, des XI. *Edict*, wegen der in Teutschland einschleichenden Schwermereyen vom 6, Octobr, 1694.

Hoch-Fürstl. Durchl. Hertzog Eberhard Ludwigs von Würtenberg, *Edict* und Verordnung, wegen der Pietisterey. *Publiciret* den 28. Februarii, Anno 1694.

Hoch-Fürstl. Durchl. Hertzog Friederichs zu Sachsen-Gotha Manifest und Verordnung wegen der so genannten Pietisterey. *Publiciret* den 4. Februarii, Anno 1697.

Desgleichen Hoch-Furstl. Durchl. zu Sachsen-Gotha gnädigste *Resolution*, auff Dero hochlöblichen Land-Stande des Furstenthums Altenburg bey dem Anno 1698 den 3 Nov. angestellten Land-Tage unterthänigst gethanen *Proposition*, die heimlichen *Conventicula* betreffend, und Ausschaffung der neuen Schwärmer oder so gemannten Peitisten.

Hoch-Fürstl. Durchl. Hertzog Georg Wilhelms zu Braunschweig und Lüneburg, *Edict*, und Verordnung wegen des *Sectarischen Pietismi, Quackerismi* oder anderen gefährlichen Irrthümern. *Publiciret* den 7, Jan. 1698.

Hoch-Fürstl. Durchl. der Frau *Abbatissin* zu Quedlinburg, gnädigste Verordnung wider die Verächter des öffentlichen Gottesdienstes, Beicht-Stuhls und Hochwürdigen Abendmahls. *Publiciret* den. 1, Aug. Anno 1700.

These edicts were afterwards published under a collective title:

*Quäcker-Greuel | Das ist: | Abscheuliche | auffrürische | verdammliche Irthum | Der neuen Schwermer | Welche genennet werden | Quäcker | Wie sie dieselbe in ihren Scartecken | Allarm | Standarte | Pannier | Königreich | Eckstein | und sonst schrifftlich und mündlich mit | grossem Ergerniss ausgebreitet. | Auf Anordnung Eines Edlen Hochweisen Raths | Der Stadt Hamburg | Den Einfältigen zu treuhert-*

ziger *Warnung kürtzlich gefasset | gründlich widerleget und in Druck gegeben | durch | Etliche hierzu verordnete | Des Ministerii in Hamburg | Auf Begehren hoher Personen auffs neue gedruckt | Im Jahr Christi 1702.* (*Appendix plate LIII.*)

In addition to the above official proclamations, there were also issued a number of books, pamphlets and broadsides about and against the Quakers and their scheme for colonization. We have here but a repetition of what had been the case in England, and called forth such works as:

"A Vindication of William Penn, | Proprietary of Pensilvania, from the late Aspersions | spread abroad on purpose to Defame him. With | an Abstract of several of his Letters since his | Departure from England.

Philip Ford,[191] London, 12th, 12th month, 1682-3. (*Appendix plate XVIII.*)

"A | Letter | from | Doctor More, | with | Passages out of several Letters | from Persons of good Credit, | Relating to the State and Improvement of | the Province of | Pennsilvania. | Published to prevent false Reports. | Printed in the Year 1687.[192] (*Appendix plate XXVIII.*)

These were followed by:

---

[191] Original in collection of Historical Society of Penna. Philip Ford was also a member of the original Frankfort company.

[192] Original in Carter Brown Library. This tract was republished in full in Penna. Mag. of Hist. and Biog., vol. iv, pp. 445-455.

"Some | Letters | and an | Abstract of Letters | from | Pennsylvania, | Containing | The State and Improvement of that | Province. | Published to prevent Mis-Reports. | London, 1691.[193] (*Appendix plate XXXIV.*)

A Dutch version of "No Cross no Crown," a new edition of Penn's "Frame of Government," and of Penn's "Travails" in Holland and Germany,—

"*Zonder Kruys, Geen Kroon, etc., door William Penn. Amsterdam 1687.*[194] (*Appendix plate XXIX.*)

"The Frame of the Government of Pennsylvania In America." London, 1691.[195] (*Appendix plate XXXIII.*)

"An Account of W. Penn's Travails in Holland and Germany, Anno *MDCLXXVII.* London, 1695.[196] (*Appendix plate XXXIX.*)

Among the important descriptive books of the time must be mentioned Richard Blome's "English America;" this was published in three languages, English, French and German:—and Gerard Croese's

---

[193] This work, a small quarto, gives a number of extracts from letters written from Philadelphia during the year 1690. The tract was reprinted in the Penna. Mag. of Hist., vol. iv, pp. 189-201. An original is among the *Penn Papers* in the Hist. Soc. of Penna., and with the exception of one in the Carter Brown Library is the only one known.

[194] Original in Hist. Soc of Penna. The first English edition is dated 1669. For various editions of this work, see Smith's Catalogue of Friends' Books

[195] Original at Hist. Soc. of Penna. Republished in Hazard's Reg., vol. ii, p. 113. See title of first edition 1682, appendix plate xii. The first Frame of Gov't, being found defective on several accounts, the second "frame" was established and accepted in the year 1683.

## Important Descriptive Books. 183

*Historia Quakeriana,* which was also printed in several languages:

The | Present State | Of His Majesties | Isles and Territories | In | America | . . . With New Maps of every Place, | etc. London: | Printed by H. Clark, for Dorman Newman, at the Kings-Arms in the Poultrey, 1687.[197] (Appendix plate XXX.)

L'amerique | Angloise, | ou | Description | des | Isles et Terres | du | Roi D'angleterre, | Dans | L'amerique. | Avec de nouvelles Cartes de chaque Isle & Terres. | Traduit de l'Anglois. | A Amsterdam, | Chez Abraham Wolfgang, | pres la Bourse. | M. DC. LXXXVIII. [198] (Appendix plate XXXI.)

Richardi Blome | Englisches | America, | oder | Kurtze doch deutliche | Beschreibung aller derer | jenigen Lander und Inseln | so der Cron Engeland in West-In | dien ietziger Zeit zustaendig und | unterthaenig sind. | durch eine hochberühmte Feder | aus dem Englischen übersetzt. | und mit Kupffern gezieret. | Leipzig | Bey Johann Groszens Wittbe und Erben. | Anno 1697. | [199] (Appendix plate XLIII.)

Gerardi Croesi | Historia | Quakeriana, | Sive | De vulgo dictis Quakeris, | Ab ortu illorum usque ad recens | natum schisma, | etc. Amstelodami, | Apud Henricum & Viduam | Theodori Boom, 1695. | [200] (Appendix plate XL.)

---

[196] Original at Hist. Soc. of Penna. The manuscript Journal kept by Penn during this journey, is now in the collection of Charles Roberts, Esq., of Philadelphia. See title *supra*. The first edition was printed by Sowle, 1694. Subsequent editions were issued from 1714-1835.

[197] Original in collection of Hist. Soc. of Penna. The part relating to Pennsylvania is virtually a reprint of Penn's "Further account." See Wm. Penn in America, Phila., 1888, p. 173.

[198] *Ibid.*

Berhard Croesens | *Quaker-Historie* | Von deren Ursprung | biss auf jüngsthin entstandene | Trennung; | Darinnen vornemlich von | den Hauptstiftern dieser Secte | derselben Lehrsaetzen und anderen | ihres gleichen zu dieser Zeit auf- | gebrachten Lehren erzehlet wird. | Berlin | den Johann Michael Rudigern. | *1696*.[201] (Appendix plate XLI.)

The | General History | of the | Quakers : | containing | The Lives, Tenents, Sufferings, Tryals, | Speeches, and Letters | Of all the most | Eminent Quakers, | Both Men & Women; | From the first Rise of that Sect, | down to this present Time. | etc.

Being Written Originally in Latin | By Gerard Croese. London, Printed for John Dunton, at the Raven, in Jewen-street. 1696.[202] (*Appendix plate XLII.*)

As the most curious work of the class of Anti-Quakeriana may be named a quarto in Latin and German, describing the *Philtris Enthusiasticis* or English and Dutch Quaker-powder ; wherein it was

---

[199] Original in Carter Brown Library. The German edition is extremely scarce.

[200] Specimens of original edition are extremely rare. Copies are in Library of German Society of Philadelphia, and of the writer. A second Latin edition 1696, is more frequently met with ; a specimen is in the Historical Society of Penna., and Phila. Lib. For a full account of Gerard Croese and his works, see "The German Pietists of Provincial Pennsylvania," Phila., 1895, pp. 43-48.

[201] The same remarks in regard to the 1695 Latin edition apply to the German edition. The only known copy in America, is the one in Library of the writer. A Dutch edition was also printed, this also is very rare, no copy is known to be in this country.

[202] Original in the collection of Charles Roberts, Esq. There is also a copy in Friends' Library at Philadelphia.

sought to prove that such a nostrum was actually in use by the Quakers to propagate their faith among those whom they wished to proselyte.

According to this curious book, their scheme was secretly to administer this *Philtre* or potion to any influential person, male or female, whom they thought to be a desirable acquisition. Within a short time such person, it was stated, commenced to tremble, and soon reached an ecstatic state, when a conversion to Quakerism was complete. Several affidavits are further cited in the work by the author, to prove that such was actually the method used to extend the faith of George Fox in Germany. As books of this kind pleased the popular fancy, they frequently had a large circulation, and went through several editions, but at the present time they are exceedingly scarce and rarely met with. The copy in possession of the writer, bears the imprint of the university of Rostock, and reads :

"*Dissertatio Historico Theologica de Philtris En-thusiasticis Anglico Batavis, etc.* . . . *Rostochl, Typis Joh. Weppling. I, Seren. Princ. & Acad. Typog.*[203] (*Appendix plate LVI.*)

The mass of literature circulated against the Quakers, however, had little or no effect upon the impending exodus from Germany.

In the year 1690, there was issued by Penn a Broadside, having for its object the settlement of

---

[203] Copy in Library of the writer.

another large city upon the banks of the Susquehanna; it was entitled:

" Proposals for a second settlement in the Province of Pennsylvania." It was a single sheet and bore the imprint : " Printed and sold by Andrew Sowle, at the crooked Billet in Halloway Lane, Shore-Ditch, 1690."

Whether the design was partially accomplished, where the proposed city was to be located, or what was the reason for his relinquishing the plan, remains an unsolved problem. The only known copy of this Broadside was formerly in the collection of the late Peter Force of Washington, D. C. It bore the marks of age and dilapidation but was in a perfect condition.[204]

At this period the position of Penn and Furly was further strengthened in Germany by the publication of several missives and tracts from Pastorius and others in Pennsylvania, setting forth the advantages of the new country in glowing terms.

The first volume upon this list is a duodecimo, containing four " Useful tracts " by Daniel Francis Pastorius; it really only advertises the Province upon the title page :

*Vier kleine | Doch ungemeine | Und sehr nutzliche| Tractätlein | . . . . Durch | Franciscum Danielem | Pastoriun. J. U. L. | Aus der In—Pensylvania neulichst von mir in | Grund angelegten und nun mit gutem | Success aufgehenden Stadt : | Germanopoli | Anno Christi M. DC. XC. |* [205] (*Appendix plate XXXII.*)

The earliest tract which really gives an extended account of the Province, was written by Pastorius in 1686, and sent to his parents in Germany. This was incorporated by Melchior Adam Pastorius, father of the Germantown pioneer, in a historical sketch of his native town of Windsheim:

*Kurtze | Beschreibung | Des H. R. Reichs Stadt | Windsheim | etc. . . . Durch | Melchiorem Adamum Pastorium, | ältern Burgemeistern und Ober-Rich- | tern in besagter Stadt. | Gedruckt zu Nürnberg | bey Christian Sigmund Froberg. | Im Jahr Christi 1692.*[206] (*Appendix plate XXXV.*)

The appendix to this work bore the following heading:

*Francisci Danielis Pastorii | Sommerhusano-Franci. | Kurtze Geographische Beschreibung | der letztmahls erfundenen | Americanischen Landschafft | Pensylvania, | Mit angehenckten einigen notablen Bege- | benheiten und Bericht-Schreiben an dessen Hrn. | Vattern Patrioten und gute Freunde.* | (*Appendix plate XXXVI.*)

This description of the Province was reprinted in various periodicals and magazines of the day,[207] and circulated extensively among the yeomanry of Germany.

---

[204] Reprinted in Hazard's Register of Pennsylvania, vol. i, p. 400, June 21, 1828. Also in North American and United States Gazette, Phila., October 25, 1848.

[205] Original in Historical Society of Penna. This volume is dedicated to Tobias Schumberg in Windsheim, a former tutor of Pastorius.

[206] Original in Historical Society of Penna.

[207] *Ibid.*

A SHIP OF THE PERIOD DURING THE FIRST GERMAN EMIGRATION.*

---

*NOTE.—It was necessary for the vessels to be armed on account of the wars on the Continent, and Freebooters at sea.

The next important issues relating to Pennsylvania of which we have any definite knowledge, was an account of Pennsylvania printed in the city of Philadelphia:

A Short | Description | of | Pennsilvania, | [208] Or, A Relation What things are known, | enjoyed, and like to be discovered in | in the said Province. | and as a Token of Good Will ———of England. | By Richard Frame. | Printed and sold by William Bradford in | Philadelphia, 1692. | (*Appendix plate XXXVII.*)

Of equal importance was the Missive or Report by Johann Gottfried Seelig to August Herman Francke, one of the fathers of Pietism, dated " *Germandon* in Pennsylvania, America d. 7, August, 1694," giving an account of the voyage and condition of the German Pietists who had left Germany in a body two years previously, and emigrated to Pennsylvania under the leadership of Magister Johann Kelpius, with the avowed intention of spreading here the Gospel of Christ and awaiting the millennium, which some of them believed was imminent. This work, a quarto, was published for circulation in Germany early in 1695, it is without an imprint, but was presumably printed either at Halle or Frankfort, and freely circulated in Pietistical circles.[209]

---

[209] Originals of this rare tract are at the Historical Society of Penna. Also, in Library of the *Weisenhaus* (Francke institution) at Halle. This missive has heretofore been attributed to Daniel Falckner. But by the Spener-Francke correspondence it is shown that the missive was sent by Seelig to Francke. The original is still in existence, from which a

*Copia | Eines Send-Schreibens aus | der neuen Welt, betreffend | etc. Christi im Jahr, 1695. (Appendix plate XXXVIII.)*

Two years later, 1697, a German edition of Blome's English America, was printed at Leipzig. (*Appendix plate XLIII.*)

It is supposed that the Hochberühmte Feder, mentioned upon the title was none other than Benjamin Furly.

At this period the list of local issues was augmented by several curious original contributions of a controversial nature, written in America, and circulated in Holland and Germany with a view to influence the Germans either for or against the followers of Spener who were attempting to introduce and maintain orthodox forms of religion in the Province.

The first of these tracts of which we have any definite knowledge was printed by Bradford in New York, for Heinrich Bernhard Köster:

"*Ein Bericht an Alle Bekenner und Schrifftsteller, 1697.*" [210]

This book, printed in the year 1696 or early in 1697, has the distinction of being the first German book printed in North America. No copy of it is known to exist; our knowledge about it is derived

---

MSS. copy was lately made for the writer. This correspondence is of the greatest importance, as it proves the connection between the Pietists in Pennsylvania with the parent organization at Halle. Above facts were not known when the "German Pietists" was written, and the authorship is there laid with Falkner. A translation of the tract by the late Dr. Oswald Seidensticker, was published in Penna. Mag. of Hist. and Biog., vol. xi, p. 430, *et seq.* See also Cramer Beiträge, p. 323.

from Pastorius's so-called "Rebuke" to Köster, in which he cites the book and states that it was printed in the High-Dutch tongue for circulation in Germany.

To counteract the influences of Köster's report in Germany and Pennsylvania, Pastorius prepared two counter-pamphlets, one for use abroad, and the other for local circulation:

Ein | Send-Brieff | Offenhertziger Liebsbezeugung an die | so genannte Pietisten in Hoch-|Deutschland. | Zu Amsterdam, | Gedruckt vor Jacob Claus Buchhändler, 1697.[211] (*Appendix plate XLIV.*)

Only a single copy of this book is known, now in possession of one of the descendants of Pastorius. As will be noticed from the title-page which is reproduced in fac-simile,[211a] it bears an European imprint. Pastorius was unable to have it done in Pennsylvania, because there was no press here at that time, so he was obliged to send the work to Holland for publication, as he had done upon several previous occasions.

The title of the tract in the English language, for home circulation, was:

Henry Bernhard Koster, William Davis, | Thomas Rutter & Thomas Bowyer, | Four | Boasting Disputers | Of this World briefly | Rebuked, | etc. Printed and Sold by William Bradford at the | Bible in New York, 1697. | [212] (*Appendix plate XLV.*)

---

[210] German Pietists of Prov. Penna; p. 287, *et seq.*
[211] Original in private hands. Page 15 closes with colophon: *Von*

Leaving the controversial works, and turning our attention once more to the literature relating exclusively to the German emigration, we now come to:

An Historical and Geographical Account | of the | Province and Country | of | Pensilvania | and of | West-New-Jersey | in | America. | With a Map of both Countries. | By Gabriel Thomas, | who resided there about Fifteen Years. | London, Printed for, and Sold by A. Baldwin, at | the Oxon Arms in Warwick-Lane, 1698. | [213] (*Appendix plate XLVI.*)

A German translation of this book was soon after published by the Frankfort company:

*Pensylvaniæ | Beschrieben von | Gabriel Thomas | 15. Jähringen Inwohner dieses | Landes | Franckfurt und Leipzig, | Zu finden bey Andreas Otto, | Buchhändlern.*[214] (*Appendix plate XLVII.*)

Pastorius's extended account of the Province comes next in order:

*Umständige Georgra- | phische | Beschreibung | Der zu allerletzt erfundenen | Provintz | Pensylva- | niæ, | In denen End-Græntzen | Americæ | In der West-Welt gelegen | Durch | Franciscum Danielem | Pastorium, | J. V. Lic. und Friedens-Richtern | daselbsten. | Worbey angehencket sind eini- | ge notable Begebenheiten, und | Bericht-Schreiben an dessen Herrn | Vattern | Melchiorem Adamum Pasto- | rium, | Und andere gute Freunde. | Franckfurt und Leipzig, | Zufinden bey Andreas Otto. 1700.* | [215] (*Appendix plate XLVIII.*)

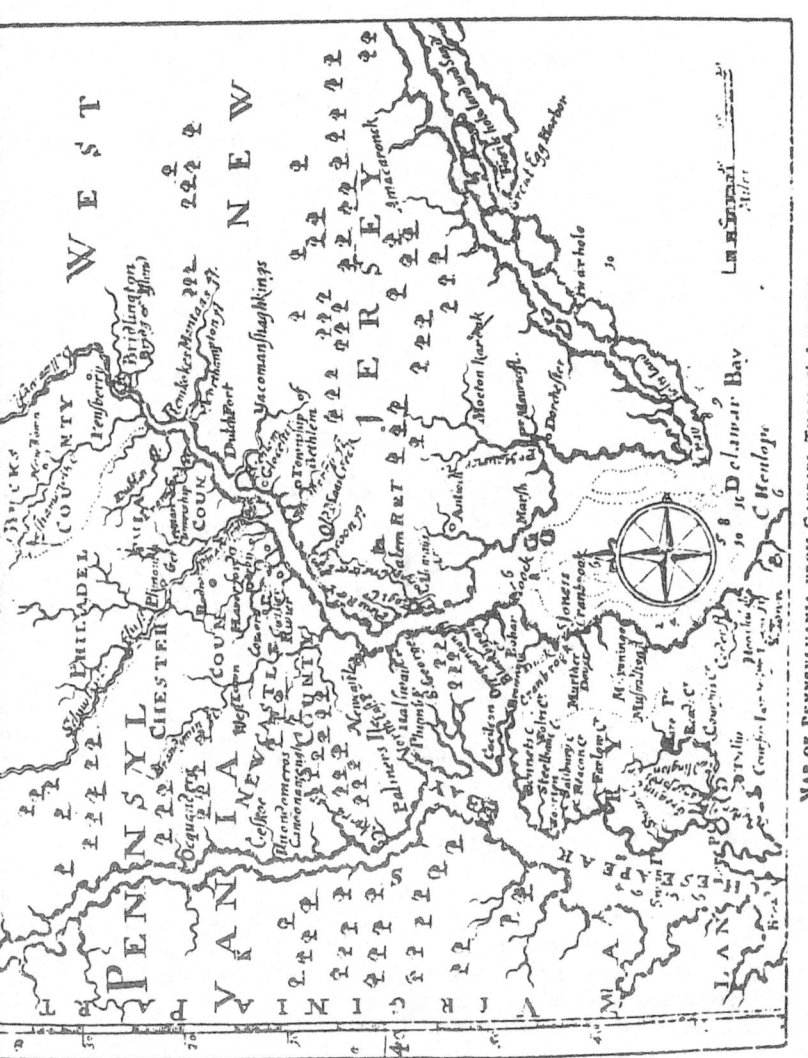

MAP OF PENNSYLVANIA FROM GABRIEL THOMAS' ACCOUNT.

An abstract and review of the above was printed in the:

*Monathlicher | Auszug | aus | allerhand neu-herausge | gebenen, nützlichen und artigen | Büchern. | December M. D CC. | Zu finden | Bey Nicol. Förstern, Buchhändl. | in Hanover.*[216] (*Appendix plate XLIX.*)

In the following year, 1701, was issued another German edition of William Penn's Letter to the king of Poland. This was circulated in north-eastern Germany, and was intended to spread the Quaker faith in that state, and at the same time induce a further emigration to the province:

*Brief | Aan den | Koning van Poolen. | Opgestelt door | William Penn, | Uyt de Naam van zijn verdrukte enlydende Vrienden | tot Dantzig. | Uit het Engelsch vertaald | Door | P. V. M. | t'Amsteldam, | By Jacob Claus, | Boekverkoper in de Prince-straat. 1701.* |[217] (*Appendix plate L.*)

---

*Eurem liebgeneigten Freund Frantz Daniel Pastorius.* Germantown in Pennsylvania, *den letzten December, 1696.* A fac-simile reproduction of the whole tract, by the writer is in the collection of Historical Society of Penna., State Library, Hon. Sam'l W. Pennypacker and the writer.

[211a] Appendix plate XLIV.

[212] Original at Friends' Library, Phila. Also one copy in private hands. Fac-simile, *ibid supra*.

[214] This was published separately and later incorporated in Pastorius's extended geographical account, edition 1704.

[215] Original at Historical Society of Penna. This book was edited by Melchior Adam Pastorius, father of the writer.

[216] Original in Historical Society of Penna.

[217] Original in Carter Brown Library.

The next important works of the period, are Daniel Falckner's "Curious Information," which he had placed with the publishers during his visit to Germany, 1698-1700;[218] and his brother's missive from Germantown:

*Curieuse Nacnricht | von|Pensylvania | in | Norden-America |welche|Auf Begehren guter Freunde| Uber vorgelegte 103. Fra- | gen bey seiner Abreiss aus Teutsch|land nach obigem Lande Anno 1700. | ertheilet und nun Anno 1702 in den Druck | gegeben worden. | Von|Daniel Falknern, Professore, | Burgern und Pilgrim allda. | Franckfurt und Leipzig,| zufinden bey Andreas Otto, Buchhändlern | Im Jahr Christi 1702.*[219] (*Appendix plate LI.*)

The Missive of Justus Falckner, a brother of the above, who accompanied him to America, was a letter to a clerical friend in Holstein, which, as it states upon the title, is an account of the religious condition of the Province in the years 1700-1. But a single copy of this work is known:[220]

*Abdruck | Eines Schreibens | An | Tit. Herrn | D. Henr. Muhlen, | Aus Germanton, in der Ameri|canischen Province Pensylvania, sonst No-|va Suecia, den ersten Augusti, im Jahr | unsers Heyls eintausend siebenhundert | und eins, | Den Zustand der Kirchen | in America betreffend.| MDCCII.* (*Appendix plate LII.*)

---

[218] German Pietists of Prov. Penna. Phila., 1895, pp. 93-99. 299-334.
[219] *Ibid*, pp. 98-9. Original in Historical Society of Penna.
[220] This heretofore unknown tract on Pennsylvania, was found by a

The list closes with two more tracts by Pastorius, the first of which is really a second edition of his former description of the Province:[221]

*Umständige Geographische | Beschreibung | Der zu allerletzt erfundenen | Provintz | Pensylva|niæ, | etc. Franckfurt und Leipzig, | Zu finden bey Andreas Otto. 1704. | (Appendix plate LIV.)*

The second one is a "continuation" of the above, to which is added Gabriel Thomas' account and Daniel Falckner's tract:[222]

*Continuatio|Der | Beschreibung der Landschafft| Pensylvaniæ | An denen End-Gräntzen | Americæ. | Uber vorige des Herrn Pastorii | Relationes. | In sich haltend : | Die Situation, und Fruchtharkeit des | Erdbodens. Die Schiffreiche und andere | Flüsse. Die Anzahl derer bisshero gebauten Städte. | Die seltsame Creaturen an Thieren, Vögeln und Fischen. | Die Mineralien und Edelgesteine. Deren eingebohrnen wilden Völcker Sprachen, Religion und Gebräuche. Und | die ersten Christlichen Pflantzer und Anbauer | dieses Landes. | Beschrieben von | Gabriel Thomas | 15 Jährigen Inwohner dieses | Landes. | Welchem Tractætlein noch beygefüget sind : | Des Hn. Daniel Falckners | Burgers und Pilgrims in Pensylvania 193. | Beantwortungen uff vorgelegte Fragen von | guten Freunden. | Franckfurt und Leipzig, | Zu finden bey Andreas Otto, Buchhændlern. | (Appendix plate LV.)*

As will be seen from the title-pages, the tracts of both Pastorius and Daniel Falckner were published simultaneously at Frankfort and Leipzig, under the auspices of the Frankfort Land Company.[223] They were repeatedly reprinted and quoted in the periodicals and reviews of the day. One of such reviews is now in the Historical Society's collection.[224]

This literature did much to influence German emigration to America, and after events showed that the printing-press in Germany was one of the most active factors in bringing about the German settlement of Pennsylvania.

When fairly started, the effects of this movement were phenomenal; the romantic Rhine became the chief artery of travel for the stream of emigrants to Pennsylvania. As the barges floated down the river past castle-crowned crag and vine-clad hill, from every hamlet could be heard the *Lebe-wohl*, and *Geht-mit-Gott*, which were called after the wanderers.

Rotterdam henceforth became the chief port of embarkation for a large portion of the Germans going to the new world, whether directly or by way of England.

---

correspondent of the writer, in the Library of the University at Rostock, after great difficulty a photographic copy of the whole was obtained, a reproduction of which is at the Historical Society of Penna. A translation made by the writer will be published in the Penna. Mag. in the near future. For Biographical sketch of Justus Falckner, refer to German Pietists of Prov. Penna., pp. 341-385. Also Lutheran Church Review, vol. xvi, p. 283, *et seq.*

[221] Original in Historical Society of Penna.

[222] *Ibid*, to this are added, Gabriel Thomas' description of Pennsylvania, and Daniel Falckner's tract, *Curieuse nachricht*, etc.

[223] See William Penn in America, Phila. 1888, pp. 304-5.

[224] *Monathlicher Auszug*, Hanover 1700.

This desire grew among the German peasantry, until it assumed such proportions that both England and the States-General were forced to take heroic measures to turn back the human tide, which not only threatened to depopulate some provinces in Germany, but also to change Pennsylvania into a German colony.

*Julius F. Sachse*

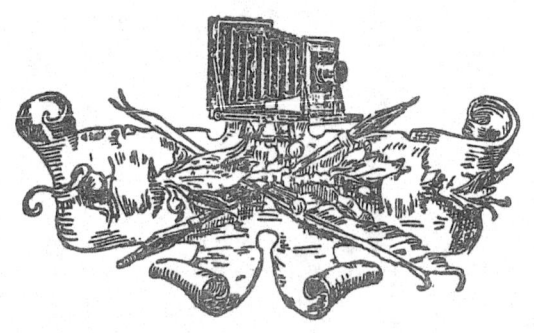

## POSTSCRIPT.

After the above paper was written and put into print, several letters, dating from the closing years of the last century, were discovered which have caused some doubt to arise in my mind as to the identity of the Dr. Otto who sent the communication "On the Discovery of America" to Dr. Franklin, by him presented to the American Philosophical Society and subsequently printed in the Transactions.

In the course of this Monograph, following the traditions of the Society, the credit of authorship is given to *Dr. John Matthew Otto*, of Bethlehem, a member of the Society and a friend of Franklin, who always signed his name "Otto" or "Dr. Otto," as in the communication read before the Society.

From the letters alluded to, it appears that at the same period (1786) there was another person of similar name, *Louis Gillaume* [sic] *Otto*, the French Minister to the United States, who was also a friend and correspondent of Franklin, and signed himself "Otto." However, it matters but little whether the writer was the learned Doctor of Bethlehem or the French Minister in New York; the facts remain the same, viz., that the paper quoted formed the incentive for the critical investigations of Baron Humboldt into the early history of America.

JULIUS F. SACHSE.

*October, 1897.*

Julius Friedrich Sachse

# APPENDIX.

## TITLE PAGES

OF

## BOOK AND PAMPHLETS

THAT INFLUENCED

## German Emigration

TO

## Pennsylvania

REPRODUCED IN FAC-SIMILE

FOR

The Pennsylvania=German Society.

BY

JULIUS FRIEDRICH SACHSE.

PHILADELPHIA.
1897.

[1675]   *Appendix.*   201

# Send-Brieff

An

## Die Bürgermeister und Raht

der Stadt

# DANZIG,

Von

**WILHELM PENN,**

aus London neulich geschrieben/

Und aus diesen Landen denen obgesetzten zugesandt:

Nun aber

Offentlich gedruckt/ zu dem Ende/ daß alle/ vornemlich die Gewaltigen auff Erden/ und die (so genanten) Geistlichen / bey sich erwegen mögen/ wie viel und welcherley ungereimte und schädliche Dinge erfolgen aus den n Gründen/ welche andere wegen der Religion, und derselben offentlichen und freyen übung zu verfolgen / gebraucht werden.

---

In Amsterdam.

Gedruckt bey **Christoff Cunraden.** Anno 1678.

Plate I.—Title-page of Penn's Missive to the Burgomaster and Council of the city of Danzig.

## Forderung der Christenheit fürs Gericht:

### Sampt

Einer freundlichen Heymsuchung in der Liebe Gottes/ an alle die jenige unter allerley Secten und Religionen, welche eine Begierde und Verlangen haben nach der Wahren Erkändtnüß Gottes/ auff daß sie ihm in der Warheit und Gerechtigkeit mochten dienen und anbeten/ sie seyn auch wie sie wollen.

### Wie auch

Ein Sendbrieff an alle die jenige/ die unter der Christlichen Confession, und von den äußerlichen Secten und Gemeinden oder Kirchen abgesondert sind.

### Und auch zuletzt

Ein Sendbrieff an alle die jenige die von dem Tag ihrer Heymsuchung empfindlich seyn geworden.

Welches alles in Englischer Sprache geschrieben ist

von

WILHELM PENN,

und in die Hochteutsche Sprache treulich transferiret.

In Amsterdam/
Gedruckt vor Jacob Claus, Anno 1678.

Plate II.—German title-page of Penn's "Call to Christendom."

Eine

**Freundliche Heymsuchung**

in der

**Liebe Gottes,**

welche die Welt überwindet.

An alle diejenigen, die ein Verlangen haben,
GOtt zu kennen, und ihn in Warheit und Auff=
richtigkeit anzubitten, von was Secte, oder
Art von Gottesdienst dieselbigen in der gan=
tzen (so genanten) Christenwelt seyn mögen,
und vornemlich in Hoch= und Nieder=
Teutschland.

Begreiffende

Ein klar Gezeugnüs zu dem alten Apostolischen
Leben, Weg, und Anbetung im Geist und in der
Warheit; die Gott in dieser Zeit auf der Erde
wiederum auffrichten, und lebendig
machen.

In Amsterdam,
Gedruckt vor Jacob Claus, Anno 1678.

Plate III—German title-page to Penn's "Tender Visitation."

# Het CHRISTENRIJK TEN OORDEEL gedagvaart.

Een tedere befoekinge in de Liefde Gods, aan alle die gene die een begeerte hebben om God te kennen en hem in Waarheyd en Opregtigheyd aan te bidden, van wat Sekte, of foort van Godsdienst de felve zouden mogen wefen

Een Missive aan alle die gene, die, onder de belyders der Christelijkheyd, afgefondert zijn van de fichtbare Sekten, en *uyterlijke* Gemeenten.

EN

Een Missive aan al die gene, die gevoelig zijn van den dag hárer befoekinge.

*Alles in d'Engelfe Tale gefchreven,* door

## WILLIAM PENN.

En daar uyt overgefet.

---

Tot ROTTERDAM.
Gedrukt voor JAN PIETERSZ GROENWOUT, Boekverkooper, wonende op het Speuy 1678

Plate IV.—Fac-simile of the Dutch collective title-page of Penn's Tracts. Original in the "Archief der Gemeente," Rotterdam.

# SOME
# ACCOUNT
### OF THE
# PROVINCE
### OF
# PENNSILVANIA
### IN
# AMERICA;

Lately Granted under the Great Seal

OF

# ENGLAND
### TO
# William Penn, &c.

Together with Priviledges and Powers necef-
fary to the well-governing thereof.

Made publick for the Information of such as are or may be
difpofed to Tranfport themfelves or Servants
into thofe Parts.

---

*LONDON*: Printed, and Sold by *Benjamin Clark*
Bookfeller in *George-Yard Lombard-ftreet*, 1681.

Plate V.—Reduced fac-simile of title-page.

Eine

# NACHRICHT

wegen der Landschaft

# PENNSILVANIA

in

# AMERICA:

Welche
Jüngstens unter dem Grossen Siegel
in

# ENGELLAND

an

# William Penn, &c.

Sambt den Freyheiten und der Macht / so zu behöriger
guten Regierung derselben nötig /
ubergeben worden /
und

Zum Unterricht derer / so etwan bereits bewogen / oder noch
möchten bewogen werden / sind sich selbsten darhin
zu begeben / oder einige Bediente und Gesinde
an diesen Ort zu senden / hiermit
kund gethan wird.

Aus dem in London gedrucktem und albar bey Benjamin Clarck
Buchhändlern in George-Yard Lombard-street befindlichem
Englischen übergesetzet.

Nebenst beygefügtem ehemaligem im 1675. Jahr gedrucktem
Schreiben des oberwehnten Will. Penns.

---

Ju Amsterdam / gedruckt bey Christoff Cunraden,
Im Jahr 1681.

Plate VI.—German title-page of Penn's "Some Account of the Province."

Een kort Bericht
*Van de Provintie ofte Landschap*
# PENN-SYLVANIA
genaemt, leggende in
# AMERICA;
Nu onlangs onder het groote Zegel van Engeland
gegeven aan
## WILLIAM PENN, &c.
*MITSGADERS*
Van de Privilegien, ende Macht om
het selve wel te Regeeren.

Uyt het Engels overgeset na de Copye tot Londen gedrukt by *Benjamen Clark*, Boekverkooper in George Yard Lombardstreet, 1681.

Waer by nu gevoegt is de Notificatie van s' Konings Placcaets in date van den 2 April 1681, waer inne de tegenwoordige Inwoonders van PENN-SYLVANIA, belast word Willem Penn en zijn Erfgenamen, als volkomene Eygenaars en Gouverneurs, te gehoorsamen.

*Als mede,*

De Copye van een Brief by den selven W.P. geschreven aan zekere Regeeringe Anno 1675. tegens de Vervolginge en voor de Vryheyt van Conscientie, aan alle &c.

---

Tot ROTTERDAM,
Gedrukt by Pieter van Wynbrugge, Boek-Drukker in de
Leeuwestraat, in de Wereld Vol-Druk. Anno 1681.

Plate VII.—Fac-simile of Dutch title-page of Penn's "Some Account of the Province." [From the original in Carter Brown Library, through courtesy of John Nicholas Brown.]

# LIBERTY OF CONSCIENCE

Upon its true and proper Grounds
ASSERTED & VINDICATED.

PROVING,

That no Prince, nor State, ought by force to compel Men to any part of the Doctrine, Worship, or Discipline of the Gospel.

To which is added, The SECOND PART;
VIZ.

## Liberty of Confcience,

The Magiftrates Intereft;

OR,

To grant *Liberty of Confcience* to perfons of *different perfwafions* in matters of *Religion*, is the great Intereft of all Kingdoms and States, and particularly of *England*; Afferted and proved.

By a PROTESTANT, a lover of Truth, and the Peace and Profperity of the Nation.

The *Second Edition*, corrected by the Author, with fome Addition.

*London*, Printed in the Year, 1668.

Plate VIII.—Title-page of Penn's "Liberty of Conscience." A translation of which was printed in the two previous tracts.

GEOGRAPHIÆ UNIVERSALIS
PARS PRIOR.

Das ist:
Der allgemeinen
Erd-Beschreibung
Erster Theil/
Darinnen die Drey Theil der Welt/
Nemlich
America/Africa/und Asia/
Samt ihren vornehmsten Königreichen/ Län-
dern/ Inseln/ Städten und Schlössern/ wie auch
Land-Charten und Wappen/ nebenst-denen sich da
selbst so wol vor langer als kurzer Zeit zugetragenen
denk-und noch heutiges Tages sehenswürdi-
gen Sachen auf das deutlichste ent-
halten.
Anfangs in Französischer Sprach
beschrieben durch P. du Val. Ihrer Königl.
Maj in Franckreich Geogr. Ordin.

Anjetzo aber ins Teutsche übersetzet/und
in dieser zweyten Edition an unterschiedlichen
Orten/ wo es die Noth erfordert/ fast um die
Helffte vermehret/
von Johann Christoff Beer.

Nürnberg
In Verleg. Johann Hoffmañs Buch-
und Kunsthändlers/
Gedruckt daselbst bey Christian Sieg-
mund Froberg.
M. DC. LXXXI.

**Plate IX.**—Title page of Du Val's Geography (German translation).
From the original in Carter Brown Library.

# RECIT
## DE
# L'ESTAT
## PRESENT
### DES
### CELEBRES COLONIES

De la Virginie, de Marie-Land, de la Caroline, du nouveau Duché
d'York, de Penn-Sylvania, & de la nouvelle Angleterre, situées
dans l'Amerique septentrionale, entre les trente deuxiéme
& quarante sixiéme degrés de l'élevation du Pole du
Nord, & établies sous les auspices, & l'autorité
souveraine du Roy de la grand' Bretagne.

*Tiré fidelement des memoires des habitans des mêmes Colonies,
en faveur de ceux, qui auroyent le dessein de s'y
transporter & de s'y établir.*

A ROTTERDAM,
Chez REINIER LEERS,
M. DC. LXXXI.

Plate X.—From the original in Carter Brown Library, through courtesy of John Nicholas Brown.

# THE ARTICLES, Settlement and Offices Of the FREE SOCIETY OF TRADERS IN PENNSILVANIA:

Agreed upon by divers MERCHANTS And OTHERS for the better Improvement and Government OF TRADE IN THAT PROVINCE.

LONDON,
Printed for Benjamin Clark in George-Yard in Lombard-street, Printer to the Society of Pennsilvania, MDCLXXXII.

Plate XI.—Reduced fac-simile of title-page.

## The FRAME of the
# GOVERNMENT
### OF THE
## Province of Pennsilvania
### IN
# AMERICA:

Together with certain

# LAWS

Agreed upon in England
### BY THE
# GOVERNOUR
### AND
## Divers FREE-MEN of the aforesaid PROVINCE.

To be further Explained and Confirmed there by the first *Provincial Council* and *General Assembly* that shall be held, if they see meet.

---

Printed in the Year MDCLXXXII.

Plate XII.—Title-page of Penn's "Frame of Government."

# Information and Direction

TO

Such Persons as are inclined

TO

# AMERICA,

MORE

Especially Those related to the Province

OF

# PENNSYLVANIA.

That the Value and Improvement of *Estates* in our Parts of *America*, may yet appear with further clearness and Assurance to Enquirers, I propose to speak my own Knowledg; and the Observation of others, as particularly as I can; which I shall comprise under these Heads.

I. The *Advance that is upon Money and Goods*
II. The *Advance that is upon Labour, be it of Handicrafts or others.*
III. The *Advance that is upon Land*
IV. The *Charge of Transporting a Family, and Fitting a Plantation*
V. The *Way the Poorer sort may be Transferred and Seated, with Advantage to the Rich that help them.*
VI. The *easier and better provision that is to be made there for Posterity, especially by those that are not of great Substance.*
VII. *What Utensils and Goods are fitting to carry for Use or Profit*

For the first, Such *Money* as may be carried, as pieces of eight, advances *Thirty*, and *Goods* at least *Fifty per cent*. Say I have 100 *l. sterl*. If I am but six in Family, I will pay my Passage with the advance upon my money, and find my hundred pounds good in the Country at last. Upon *Goods*, well bought and sorted, there is more profit: but some money is very requisit for Trade sake: for we find it gives Goods a better market, to those considering the great quantity of Goods already carried, it were not amiss at present, if one half were in *Money*, and the other in *Goods*.

Thus in General: But it particularly encourages Merchants because the profit by advance, is seldom less then 50 *l. per cent*, which is very considerable, and we have already got some things for returns as *Skins, Furrs, Whale Oyle, Tobacco* &c.

II. For *Labour*, be it of *Handicrafts, or Others*, there is a considerable Encouragement by advance of price, to what is here, because the Goods Manufactured there,

III. The *Advance* upon *Land* is Encouraging, which will be best apprehended by an English understanding in a Comparison with the Lands of *England*, that he is familiarly acquainted with.

If 500 Acres of *uncleard* Land there, indifferently chosen, will *keep as many Milch Cowes, or fat as many Bullocks* for the market in Summer, as 50 Acres of improved Land in *England*, as chosen aforesaid, can do, then by Computing the value of the Summers Grass of such fifty Acres of Land here, we shall the better find the value of 500 Acres of Land in *America*; for within that compass, the same quantity of Cattle may be well kept. Admit this then, that the Summers Grass of 50 Acres of midling Land in *England*, is worth 15 *l*. I conceive that makes 20 *l*. which is the price of the Inheritance of the 500 Acres, no dear Purchas. The cost to go thither is no Objection, because it is paid by the *Advance* that is upon the Money and Goods at the rate aforesaid. If the hazard of the Seas be Objected, we see that the *five hundreth* Ship using those parts, does not miscarry, and the Risk is run to themselves only. However, except in Winter, Passages are pleasant, as well as safe.

But this Comparison draws an Objection upon us that must be obviated. That Incomes of your *flock in the Winter*? I say our *Woods* usually keep them for the Market till *December*, and unless it be a more then ordinary Winter (which is observed to happen but once in four or five Years, or that they are young flock, or Cattel big with Young, they mostly shift for themselves. But if Fodder be wanted, we have a supply by *Hay*, we mow in the *Marshes* and *Woods*, or the *Straw* of the English Grain we use, or the *Tops and Stalks* of Indian Corn, and sometimes that it self; a Thing *hearty, and easily rais'd*, and is good to fat as well as keep: and answers to *Oats, Pease, Beans and Fetches* here; though we have them also.

This Scheam of *Grazing and keeping* of Stock, may inform Inquirers what the Woods and unbroken Lands of those Countrys in some sort will do in proportion to Lands here, and consequently, what they are worth to Lands

Plate XIII.—This Tract, written by Penn, is of the greatest rarity and of interest as exhibiting the terms upon which Penn disposed of his lands.

( 1. )

# Nader Informatie of Onderrechtinge voor de gene die genegen zijn om na AMERICA te gaan, en wel voornamentlijk voor die geene die in de Provintie van PENSYLVANIA geintrefleert zijn.

OP dat het verder blijken mach, hoe onfe goederen en landeryen, in die quartieren van America, vermeerdert en verbetert kunnen worden, fo heb ik tot meerder onderricht en verfekeringe van die geene, die daar na fouden mogen vragen, voorgenoomen aan mijn eygen ervarentheyt en kennifle in die fake, nevens de opmerkingen van andere, met foo veel omftandigheden als 't doenlijk is, voor te ftellen onder de feven navolgende hoofftftukken.

I. Het voordeel dat 'er valt op den invoer van gelt, en koopmanfchappen.
II. Het voordeel op den arbeyt, 't zy van ambachten of anders.
III. Het voordeel dat 'er is te doen, met het land felfs.
IV. Wat het koften zal om een huysgefin derwaarts te voeren, en een plantagie aan te ftellen.
V. Op wat wijfe de arme luyden fouden konnen overgevoert worden, met voordeel voor de Rijke, die haar daarin fouden behulpzaam wefen.
VI. Hoe gemakkelijker, en bequamer dat men aldaar fijn nakomelingen kan verforgen, en voornamentlijk de geene, die niet feer Riik zijn.
VII. Wat voor gereetfchappen en koopmanfchappen beft zijn, om daar na toe te brengen, 't zy om felfs te gebruyken, t zy om daar met profijt te verkoopen.

1. Wat nu het eerfte Hooftftuk belangt, ftukken van achten, of Spaanfe partacons, geven 50. ten hondert avance, en koopmanfchappen wel ingekocht, 50. ten hondert, fulks dat, genoomen dat ik hadde maar 100. l. fterlings of 450. pattacons, of Rijksdaalders, indien mijn familie maar uyt 6. perfoonen beftaat, fpo fal ik de vracht-penningen uyt de winften op het gelt betaalen, en mijn 100. l. daar te lande noch hebben. Op goederen wel ingekocht, en wel geforteert, valt 'er noch meer profijt: Maar een deel in gelde is feer dienftig, om des handels wille. Want men vindt dat de waren daar door beter getrokken worden: fulks dat gemerkt de groote quantiteyt van waren alreede daar henen gevoert, het niet ongeraden is dat men tegenwoordig d'een helft in gelde, en de ander in koopmanfchappen neemt.
Dit zy genoech in 't generaal gefeyt. Maar de Cooplyuden bevinden byfonderlijk haar felven aangemoedigt door het profijt, dat felden minder is als 50. ten hondert, 't welk een groote avance is. Wy hebben ook verfcheyde faken, om in Retouren te fenden, als Vellen, Peltery, Traan, Oly, Tabak &c.
2. Wat den arbeyt of arbeyts-loon aangaat, 't zy voor ambachts-luyden, of andere daar voor is de aanmoediginge mede confiderabel, om dat men daar meer wint als hier in Engelant; Want de waren of manufaêturen, diemen daar komt te maken, worden gedebiteert voor defelve prijs als die, die by de Coopman ingevoert worden, en de levens-middelen, daar immers foo goet koop wefende als hier in Engelant, foo moeten de ambachtsluyden in America een feer goede tijt en gelegentheyt hebben, om datfe een dobbelde
A winft

A brief Account of the

# Province of Pennsylvania,

Lately Granted by the

# KING,

Under the GREAT

# Seal of England,

TO

# WILLIAM PENN

AND HIS

# Heirs and Assigns.

Since (by the good Providence of *God*, and the Favour of the *King*) a Country in *America* is fallen to my Lot, I thought it not less my Duty, then my Honest Interest, to give some publick notice of it to the World, that those of our own or other Nations, that are inclin'd to Transport Themselves or Families beyond the Seas, may find another Country added to their Choice; that if they shall happen to like the Place, Conditions, and Government, (so far as the present Infancy of things will allow us any prospect) they may, if they please, fix with me in the Province, hereafter described.

I. *The* KING'S *Title to this Country before he granted it.*

It is the *Jus Gentium*, or Law of Nations, that what ever Waste, or unculted Country, is the Discovery of any Prince, it is the right of that Prince that was at the Charge of the Discovery: Now this *Province* is a Member of that part of *America*, which the King of *Englands* Ancestors have been at the Charge of Discovering, and which they and he have taken great care to preserve and improve.

II. William

Plate XV.—Title-page of Penn's "Brief Account" of 1682.

## Kurtze Nachricht
## Von der Americanischen Landschafft Pennsilvania.

1. Es fängt an im 40. grad der Nord-breite, liegt also ungefehr wie Neapolis in Italien, und Mompellier in Franckreich. Ist 75. teutsche meilen lang/ 45. breit; die daran grentzende Provintzien sind West- und Ost-neu Jersey, Marieland und Virginien. Hat 2. grosse Flüß; nemlich Delawar, auff welchem Schiff von 200. tonnen segeln kören, und Sesquahana, der wegen Stein-klippen in die 30. meilen unschiffbar. Die Lufft ist sehr klar und lieblich. Der Sommer länger und wärmer, der Winter hingegen kürtzer und kälter als in Engeland. Das Land ist meistentheils eben, jedoch nicht gantz ohne Berg. Das seyd leicht zu pflügen / und bereits an etlichen orten angebauet. Hat frische Brunnquellen, mehr und kräfftigere Gartenfrüchte als Europa, wiewol die Europäische daselbst auch wachsen. An Wurtzeln ists über Engeland. Die von Kernen gezielte Obst-bäume tragen schon im 4ten Jahr. Sonst findet man allbar allerhand Bäume: Maulbeer, Kästi, Welsch Nuß / Eichen / Dannen / Cedern / rc. Auch unterschiedliche Ihr Zinder, und ander Holtz, zu Schiffbau, rc. An Fischen / Vögeln, und wilden Thieren hats die Fülle. Gäntz Collucmen / Enten / Rebhüner, rc. in grosser mänig. In summa, alles was zur speise dienet, überflüssig ist gefunden. Das Wildpret seet und nicht widrig: gut schweinen Fleisch, herrlichen Salat / Brodt von Weitzen und Korn, weiß und rothen Wein / trefflich Bier / rc. Diese und dergleichen nothwendige Lebensmittel kan man daselbst von den Einwohnern vor billigen Preiß haben / und wird denen neu ankommenden zu ihrem Auffenthalt wohl bezeugnet.

II. Die Haupt-Stadt Philadelphia wird am Delawar Fluß, etwan 15. Teutsche Meil vom Meer, angelegt, und sind allschon einige wackere Häuser in die Höh. In diesem Fluß ligt auch

Plate XVI.—Heading of German edition of Penn's "Brief Account."

## Plantation Work

### THE
# WORK
### OF THIS
# GENERATION.

Written in True-Love

To all such as are weightily inclined to Transplant themselves and Families to any of the *English* Plantations in

# AMERICA.

### THE

Most material Doubts and Objections against it being removed, they may more cheerfully proceed to the Glory and Renown of the God of the whole Earth, who in all Undertakings is to be looked unto, Praised and Feared for Ever.

---

*Aspice venturo lætetur ut India Sæclo.*

*LONDON*, Printed for *Benjamin Clark* in George-Yard in Lombard-street, 1682.

Plate XVII.—Title-page of "Plantation Work." [For proof of authorship see "William Penn in America," Philadelphia, 1888, pp. 55-56.]

# A Vindication of WILLIAM PENN, Proprietary of *Pensilvania*, from the late Aspersions spread abroad on purpose to Defame him. With an Abstract of several of his Letters since his Departure from *England*.

WILLIAM PENN having been of late Traduced as being a Papist, and likewise being Dead, I thought meet to give a short Relation of the rise and ground of that slanderous Report, and Detect it, with an Abstract of his own Letters received since to shew that he is alive.

! One of the first and most furious Fomenters and Authors of that late lying Report of *William Penn*'s being a Papist (after diligent Enquiry made) appears to be *Thomas Hicks*, a Baptist Teacher, the envious false Dialogue-Maker, who has been openly prov'd a notorious Forger, Slanderer and Defamer of the Peopl. called Quakers, wickedly and maliciously rendring them no Christians, but Deceivers and Impostors, &c. and defaming them in their sufferings, which are for Conscience towards God, insinuating, That the satisfaction of their wills and lusts, and promoting their carnal Interest, to be the chief motive and Inducement thereto, and the great thing in their Eye, (as in his Dialog. 1. p.75.) As also his lies and slanders, That he had it under *W. P*'s Hand to manifest him the falsest Villain upon the Earth, and that several of his Friends had been with him to see it, and were satisfied it was so, and desired him not to look upon the rest of Friends as upon *W. P.* And further, that the Books his Name was too, were not of his own Writing, but that he kept a Jesuite for that purpose.

Now I having information of this false Report, and Slander, and being chiefly concern'd in the Affairs of *W. Penn* in his Absence, look'd upon my self oblig'd in Conscience to vindicate his Innocency and Christian Reputation: Whereupon I took with me R. *Davis* and R. M. with several others upon the *Exchange*, and asked *Tho. Hicks* if he had it under *W. Penn*'s hand to manifest him as aforesaid? To which he Answered, *Yes, he had*; Then I desired him to name one of the Friends that was so satisfied; his shuffling Answer was, There was a great many of them, but could remember the Names of none of them, it being four or five years ago. I then desired to see his Letter? He Answered, He had none. I Queried, What he had under his own Hand then? He Re——

He Answered, *The Sandy Foundation*, for which he was put in the *Tower*. Note, That an Explication was sincerely given forth by *W. Penn*, concerning the said Book, Entituled, *Innocency appearing with open Face*, which gave such satisfaction that he was set at Liberty.

So this was the substance of his Answer, by which you may perceive the feebleness of his false suggestion; and the baseness of his Spirit: then as to his gross Lye of *W. P*'s keeping a Jesuit to write his Books, when I charged him with it, to that he was Mute, and would give me no Answer, but shussled to another thing.

Hereby you may see that the said *Tho. Hicks* appears to be a busie Slanderer as well as a manifest Forger of notorious falshoods, as before charged.

The false suggestion of *Tho. Hicks* taking Air, did encourage others to add thereto; and amongst the several Stories this was one. That *W. Penn* perverted one Mr. *Edsaw*, a *Sussex* Gentleman, to the *Romish* Religion, who lived and died near his house. The first that I could find who was so bold to affirm this, was F. F. who quoted the Duke of *Somerset*'s Steward for his Author, to whom I applied my self, and he affirmed he Reported it not, neither knew any thing of it. That being detected, F. F. charged it upon Captin *Gratwick* of *Sussex*, Brother-in law to the said Captain *Edsaw*, to whom Messengers were sent by *W. Penn*'s Wife to know the truth thereof, and he also denied it, and said, *He would spit in the Face of any man that would charge it upon him*. This he declared before several Witnesses, and said, If she were not satisfied with what he had there declared, he would wait upon her, and give her what satisfaction she pleased under his hand, for he scorn'd to abuse so Civil a Gentleman behind his back: So the rise of that Story lodges as yet at F. F's door. And for the pretended perverted Person Captain *Edsaw*, (for so he was called) they who are desirous to be further satisfied, may enquire of the Warden of the *Fleet*, where, by the Book it doth appear the said *Robert Edsaw* was committed Prisoner to the *Fleet* for Debt the 27th of *November* 1678. and not known to go abroad after Commitment to his dying day, which was

Plate XVIII.—Heading of Philip Ford's "Vindication of William Penn."

# A LETTER FROM William Penn

Proprietary and Governour of

# PENNSYLVANIA

In America,

TO THE

# COMMITTEE

OF THE

# Free Society of Traders

of that Province, residing in London.

CONTAINING

A General Description of the said *Province,* its *Soil, Air, Water, Seasons* and *Produce,* both Natural and Artificial, and the good Encrease thereof.

Of the *Natives* or *Aborigines,* their *Language, Customs* and *Manners, Diet, Houses* or *Wigwams, Liberality, easie way* of *Living, Physick, Burial, Religion, Sacrifices* and *Cantiso, Festivals, Government,* and their order in *Council* upon Treaties for Land, *&c.* their *Justice* upon *Evil Doers.*

Of the *first Planters,* the *Dutch, &c.* and the *present Condition* and *Settlements* of the said *Province,* and *Courts* of *Justice,&c.*

To which is added, An Account of the CITY of

# PHILADELPHIA

Newly laid out.

Its Scituation between two Navigable Rivers, *Delaware* and *Skulkill,*

WITH A

Portraiture or Plat-form thereof,

Wherein the Purchasers Lots are distinguished by certain Numbers inserted.

And the Prosperous and Advantagious Settlements of the *Society* aforesaid, within the said City and Country, *&c.*

*Printed* and *Sold* by Andrew Sowle, *at the Crooked-Billet in* Holloway-Lane *in* Shoreditch, *and at several Stationers in* London, 1 6 8 3.

Plate XIX.—Title-page of Penn's letter to the "Free Society of Traders."

# MISSIVE
## VAN
## WILLIAM PENN,
Eygenaar en Gouverneur van
# PENNSYLVANIA,
## In AMERICA.

Geschreven aan de Commissarissen van de Vrye Societeyt der Handelaars, op de selve Provintie, binnen London resideerende.

### BEHELSENDE:

Een generale beschrijvinge van de voornoemde Provintie: te weten/ van hare Grond/Lucht/Water/Saisoenen en 't Product/ soo uyt de natuur als door het bouwen/ nessens de groote vermeerderinge of meenighvuldinge/ welke het Land aldaar uytgevende is.

Als mede: van de Natureellen of Inboorlingen des Lands/ haer Taal/ Gewoontens en Manieren / haer Spijsen / Huysen of Wigwams / Mildheyt / gemackelijcke manier van leven / Medicijnen / manieren van Begraaffenis / Godsdienst / Offerhanden en Gesangen / haar Hooge-feesten / Regeeringe / en ordre in hare Raden / wanneer sy met yemandt handelen ofter het verkoopen van Landeryen / &c. Nevens hare Justitie/ of Recht doen over quaatdoenders.

Mitsgaders een Bericht van de eerste Coloniers de Hollanders / &c. En van de tegenwoordige toestant en welgesteltheyt van de voornoemde Provintie en Rechtbanken / &c. aldaar.

Waar by noch gevoeght is een Beschrijving van de Hooft-Stadt
### PHILADELPHIA
Nu onlangs uytgeset, en gelegen tusschen twee Navigable Rivieren, namentlijk: tusschen *Delaware* en *Schuylkil*.

Ende een verhaal van de voorspoedige en voordeelige standt van saken van de voornoemde Societeyt binnen de voornoemde Stadt en Provintie /&c.

### AMSTERDAM,
Gedrukt voor JACOB CLAUS, Boekverkooper in de Prince-straat, 1684.

Plate XX.—Title of Dutch Edition.

# Beschreibung

### Der in AMERICA neu-erfundenen

## PROVINZ
# PENSYLVANIEN.

Derer Inwohner / Gesetz / Arth / Sitten und Gebrauch:

### Auch sämtlicher Reviren des Landes /

Sonderlich der Haupt-Stadt

# PHILA-DELPHIA,

Alles glaubwürdigst

Auß des Gouverneurs darinnen erstatteten

### Nachricht.

---

In Verlegung bey Henrich Heuß an der Banco / im Jahr 1684.

Plate XXI.—Title-page of German version. [From the original in Carter Brown Library.]

# RECÜEIL
## DE
# DIVERSES
## PIECES,
## CONCERNANT
### LA
## PENSYLVANIE.

A LA HAYE,
Chez ABRAHAM TROYEL,
Marchaud Libraire, dans la Grand Sale
de la Cour, M.DC.LXXXIV.

Plate XXII.—Title-page of "Collection of Various Pieces Concerning Pennsylvania.

## Eclaircissemens de Monsieur Furly, sur plusieurs Articles touchant l'établissement de la Pensylvanie.

### AUX ACHETEURS.

LE Gouverneur vend trois mille Acres ou portions de Terre cent livres Sterling qui valent onze cens livres d'Hollande, ou treize cens livres de France. Chaque Acre, ou portion, étant de la grandeur ou environ d'un Arpent d'Hollande; à la charge que l'Acheteur s'obligera, tant pour lui que pour les Descendans, d'en payer à perpétuité, & cela d'an en an, une rente d'un schelin Anglois, qui vaut douze sols d'Angleterre, pour chaque cent Acres, & on fera arpenter & delivrer ladite Terre ausdits Acheteurs toutefois & quantes qu'ils le souhaiteront, soit à eux-mêmes, ou à ceux qui auront procuration d'eux.

Cette Terre étant delivrée de la sorte, l'Acheteur sera tenu, dans le terme de trois ans, d'établir une famille sur chaque portion

Depuis que le Gouverneur a écrit la Lettre que vous allez voir, il en a encore envoyé d'autres en Angleterre en datte du dix Novembre 1683. stile nouveau, là où il donne à connoître le progrés des succés heureux qui arrivent dans cette Province ; & que dans ce mois il y étoit arrivé cinq Vaisseaux, entr'autres un qui a apporté beaucoup de gens de Crevelt, & des lieux circonvoisins, & du Maryland, Je suis

*Vôtre très-affectionné Ami,*

BENJAMIN FURLY.

*A Rotterdam*
*ce 6. Mars*
*1684.*

Plate XXIII.—Heading and Colophon of Furly's "Explanations to Purchasers and Renters" in the French edition.

## Good Order Established
### IN
## Pennſilvania & New-Jerſey
### IN
# AMERICA,

Being a true Account of the Country;
With its Produce and Commodities there made.

And the great Improvements that may be made by means of **Publick Store-houſes** for **Hemp**, **Flax** and **Linnen-Cloth**; alſo, the Advantages of a **Publick-School**, the Profits of a **Publick-Bank**, and the Probability of its ariſing, if thoſe directions here laid down are followed. With the advantages of publick **Granaries**.

Likewiſe, ſeveral other things needful to be underſtood by thoſe that are or do intend to be concerned in planting in the ſaid Countries,

All which is laid down very plain, in this ſmall Treatiſe; it being eaſie to be underſtood by any ordinary Capacity. To which the *Reader* is referred for his further ſatisfaction.

### By *Thomas Budd*.

### Printed in the Year 1685.

Plate XXIV.—Title-page of Budd's Tract, printed by William Bradford, Philadelphia. [See Hildeburn's "Issues of the Press in Penna.," p. 4.

Miffive van
### CORNELIS BOM,
Gefchreven uit de Stadt
### PHILADELPHIA.
In de Provintie van
### PENNSYLVANIA,
Leggende op d'Ooftzyde van de
Znyd Revier van Nieuw Nederland.
Verhalende de groote Voortgank
van de felve Provintie.
**Waer by komt**
De Getuygenis van
### JACOB TELNER.
van Amfterdam.

Tot Rotterdam gedrukt, by Pieter van
Wijnbrugge, in de Leeuweftract. 168:

Plate XXV.—Title-page of Cornelis Bom's "Account."

# A Further Account of the Province of PENSYLVANIA, and its Improvements.

### For the Satisfaction of those that are Adventurers, and Inclined to be so.

IT has I know, been much expected from me that I should give some farther Narrative of those parts of *America*, where I am chiefly interested, and have lately been; having continued there above a Year after my former *Relation*, and receiving since my return, the freshest and fullest Advices of its *Progress* and *Improvement*. But as the reason of my coming back, was a *difference* between the Lord *Baltamore* and my self, about the *Lands of Delaware*, in consequence, reputed of mighty moment to us, so I wav'd publishing any thing that might look in favour of the Country or inviting to it, whilst it lay under the Discouragement and Disreputation of that Lord's claim and pretences.

But since they are, after many fair and full hearings before the *Lords* of the *Committee* for *Plantations* justly and happily *Dismiss*, and the things agreed; and that the *Letters* which daily press me from all parts, on the subject of *America*, are so many and voluminous, that to answer them severally, were a Task too heavy, and repeated to perform, I have thought it most easie to the Enquirer, as well as my self, to make this Account *Publick*, left my silence, or a more private intimation of things, should disoblige the just inclinations of any to *America*, and at a time too, when an extraordinary Providence seems to favour its plantation, and open a Door to *Europeans* to pass thither. That then which is my part to do in this Advertisement is,

First, *To Relate our Progress, especially since my last of the Month called* August, 83.

Secondly, *The Capacity of the place for farther Improvement, in order to Trade and Commerce.*

A 2         Lastly,

Plate XXVI.—Heading of Penn's "Further Account."

[1685]     *Appendix.*

# TWEEDE
## Bericht ofte Relaas
### Van
### WILLIAM PENN,
Eygenaar en Gouverneur van de Provintie van

# PENNSYLVANIA,
## In AMERICA.

Behelfende een korte Befchrijvinge van den tegenwoordige toeftand en gelegentheid van die Colonie.

Midsgaders / een aanwijfinge op wat voor Conditien / die gene die onmachtig zijn / om haar felven te konnen transporteeren / daar-heenen fouden konnen worden gebracht / met voordeel tot de gene / die daer Penningen toe fouden verfchieten.

Uyt het Engels overgefet.

t'AMSTERDAM,

By JACOB CLAUS, Boekverkoper in de Prince-ftraat.

Plate XXVII.—Title-page of Dutch edition of Penn's "Further Account." [From the original in Carter Brown Library.]

# A LETTER

FROM

### Doctor More,

WITH

Paſſages out of ſeveral Letters from Perſons of good Credit,

Relating to the State and Improvement of the Province of

## PENNSILVANIA.

*Publiſhed to prevent falſe Reports.*

Printed in the Year 1687.

# ZONDER KRUYS
# GEEN KROON,

Of eene

## VERHANDELING

der Natuure en Tucht
van het heylig'

## KRUYSE CHRISTI:

*Vertoonende*

Dat de verloochening zyns zelfs, en het
dagelyks draagen van het Kruyfe Chrifti, de
eenige weg tot de Rufte en het Koning-
ryke Góds is.

Tót bekrachtiginge van 't welke hier bygevoegd
zyn, veele treffelyke Redenen en Voorbeelden
van vermaarde en geleerde perfoonen
der aaloude tyden.;

*Als mede*

Verfcheydene Getuygeniffen van Lieden van
Staat en Geleerdheyd, op hunne
fterf-ftonde uytgefproken.

Door

## WILLIAM PENN,

Gouverneur en Eygenaar van
*Penfylvania.*

In de Engelfche Taale befchre eren, en in de zelve eenige reyzen herdrukt, en nu daar uyt, ten dienfte ci.-
zer Lands-lieden, in 't Nederduytfch gebracht
Door

W<sup>m</sup>. Séwel.

Amfterdam, by JACOB CLAUS, Boekverkooper in de Prinfe-ftraat, 1687.

---

**Plate XXIX.**—Title-page of Dutch edition of Penn's "No Cross No Crown." Original English edition printed in the year 1669.

# THE
# Present State

Of His Majesties

## Isles and Territories
# IN
# AMERICA,
### VIZ.

Jamaica, Barbadoes, Anguilla, Bermudas,
S. Christophers, Nevis, Carolina, Virginia,
Antego, S. Vincent, New-England, Tobago.
Dominica, New-Jersey, New-Found-Land.
Pensilvania, Monserat, Mary-Land, New-York.

With *New Maps* of every Place.

Together with

*Astronomical* T A B L E S,

Which will serve as a constant *Diary* or *Calendar*, for the use of the *English* Inhabitants in those Islands; from the Year 1686, to 1700.

Also a *Table* by which, at any time of the Day or Night here in *England*, you may know what *Hour* it is in any of those parts. And how to make *Sun-Dials* fitting for all those places.

*Licens'd,* July 20. 1686. Roger L'Estrange.

*L O N D O N:*
Printed by *H. Clark*, for Dorman Newman, at the Kings-Arms in the *Poultrey*, 1687.

Plate XXX.—Title-page of Blome's "English America."

# L'AMERIQUE
## ANGLOISE,
## OU
# DESCRIPTION
### DES
## ISLES ET TERRES
### DU
## ROI D'ANGLETERRE,
### DANS
## L'AMERIQUE.

Avec de nouvelles Cartes de chaque Isle & Terres.

*Traduit de l'Anglois.*

A AMSTERDAM,
Chez ABRAHAM WOLFGANG,
prés la Bourse.

M. DC. LXXXVIII.

Plate XXXI.—French-title page of Blome's "English America."

### Vier kleine
### Doch ungemeine
### Und sehr nützliche
# Tractätlein

De omnium Sanctorum Vitis
I. De omnium Pontificum Statutis
II. De Conciliorum Decisionibus
V. De Episcopis & Patriarchis Constantinopolitanis.

Das ist:
1. Von Aller Heiligen Lebens-Ubung
2. Von Aller Päpste Gesetz-Einführung
3. Von der Concilien Stritt-Sopirung.
4. Von denen Bischöffen und Patriarchen zu Constantinopel.

Zum Grunde
Der künfftighin noch ferner darauf
zu bauen Vorhabender Warheit
præmittiret,

Durch
FRANCISCUM DANIELEM
PASTORIUN. J. U. L.

Aus der
In Pensylvania neulichst von mir in
Grund angelegten / und nun mit gutem
Success aufgehenden Stadt:
GERMANOPOLI
Anno Christi M. DC. XC.

Plate XXXII.—Title-page of Pastorius' "Four Useful Tracts."

# The FRAME OF THE GOVERNMENT

Of the *Province* of

# 𝔓𝔢𝔫𝔫𝔰𝔶𝔩𝔟𝔞𝔫𝔦𝔞

In *America.*

---

Printed, and Sold by *Andrew Sowle* at the Crooked-Billet in *Holloway-Lane* in *Shoreditch,* 1691.

**Plate XXXIII.**—Title-page second edition of Penn's "Frame of Government."

## Some
# LETTERS
### AND AN
## Abstract of Letters
### FROM
# PENNSYLVANIA,

Containing

The State and Improvement of that Province.

---

*Published to prevent Mis-Reports.*

---

Printed, and Sold by *Andrew Sowe*, at the *Crooked-Billot* in *Hollo-way-Lane*, in *Shoreditch*, 1691.

## Kurtze Beschreibung Des H. R. Reichs Stadt Windsheim/

Samt

Dero vielfältigen Unglücks-Fällen/ und wahrhafftigen Ursachen ihrer so grossen Decadenz und Erbarmungs-würdigen Zustandes/

Aus

Alten glaubwürdigen Documentis und Brieflichen Urkunden ( der itzo lebenden lieben Burgerschafft/ und Dero Nachkommen/ zu guter Nachricht) also zusammen getragen/ und in den Druck gegeben

durch

Melchiorem Adamum Paſtorium, ältern Burgemeiſtern und Ober-Richtern in besagter Stadt.

Gedruckt zu Nürnberg
bey Christian Sigmund Froberg.
Im Jahr Christi 1692.

Plate XXXV.—Title-page of Melchior Adam Pastorius' Tract on "Windsheim and Pennsylvania."

FRANCISCI DANIELIS PASTORII
Sommerhusano-Franci.
Kurtze Geographische Beschreibung
der letztmahls erfundenen
Americanischen Landschafft
PENSYLVANIA,
Mit angehenckten einigen notablen Bege=
benheiten und Bericht=Schreiben an dessen Hrn.
Vattern/ Patrioten und gute Freunde.

───────────────────

Vorrede.

ES ist denen Meinigen insgesamt zur
Gnüge bekandt/ auf was Weise ich/
von meinen Kindesbeinen an/ auf
dem Wege dieser Zeitlichkeit meinen
LebensLauff gegen die frohe Ewigkeit zu/ ein=
gerichtet und in allem meinem Thun dahin ge=
trachtet habe/ wie ich den allein guten Willen
GOttes erkennen / seine hohe Allmacht fürch=
ten / und seine unergründliche Güte lieben ler=
nen möchte. Und obwohlen ich nebst andern
gemeinen Wissenschafften der freyen Künste/
das Studium Juris feliciter absolviret / die Jta=
liänisch und Frantzösische Sprachen ex funda-
mento begriffen / auch den so genannten gros=
sen Tour durch die Landschafften gethan / so
habe ich jedoch an allen Orten und Enden mei=
nen grössesten Fleiß und Bemühung an anders
nichts gewendet/als eigentlich zu erfahren/wo
A        doch

Plate XXXVI.—Heading of description of Pennsylvania in Melchior Adam Pastorius' "Windsheim Tract."

# A Short
# DESCRIPTION
## OF
# Pennſilvania,

Or, A Relation What things are known, enjoyed, and like to be diſcovered in in the ſaid Province.

*...d ... Tok... of Good Will ... ./
of* England.

---

*By* Richard Frame.

---

*Printed and Sold by* William Bradford *in* Philadelphia, 1692.

Plate XXXVII.—Title-page from Frame's "Description of Pennsylvania." [Original in L. C. P. Presented (?) as a Token of Good Will to the People (?) of England.]

# COPIA

### Eines Send=Schreibens auß der neuen Welt/ betreffend

### Die Erzehlung einer gefährlichen Schifffarth/ und glücklichen Anländung etlicher Christlichen Reisegefehrten/ welche zu dem Ende diese Wallfahrt angetretten/ den Glauben an JEsum CHristum allda außzubreiten

Tob. XII. 8.

Der Könige und Fürsten Rath und Heimlichkeiten soll man verschweigen/ aber GOttes Werck soll man herrlich preisen und offenbaren.

Gedruckt im Jahr 1695.

**Plate XXXVIII.**—Title-page of Johann Gottfried Seelig's "Report to A. H. Francke, after his arrival in Pennsylvania."

> AN
> ACCOUNT
> OF
> **W. Penn's**
> TRAVAILS
> IN
> HOLLAND and GERMANY,
> Anno MDCLXXVII.
> For the Service of the Gospel of Christ, by way of **Journal**.
> Containing also Divers Letters and Epistles writ to several Great and Eminent Persons whilst there.
>
> **The Second Impression**, Corrected by the Author's own Copy, with Answers to some of the Letters, not before Printed.
>
> *London*, Printed and Sold by *T. Sowle*, in *White-Hart-Court* in *Grace-Church-Street*. 1695.

Plate XXXIX.—Title-page of Second Edition of "Penn's Travels in Germany."

GERARDI CROESI
# HISTORIA QUAKERIANA,

Sive

De vulgò dictis QUAKERIS,
Ab ortu illorum usque ad recèns
natum schisma,

LIBRI III.

In quibus præsertim agitur de ipso-
rum præcipuis antecessoribus, & dogmatis
(ut & similibus placitis aliorum hoc
tempore) factisque ac casibus
memorabilibu .

AMSTELODAMI,
Apud HENRICUM & Viduam
THEODORI BOOM. 1695.

Plate XL.—Title-page to original edition of Croese's "Historia Quakeriana."

Gerhard Croesens

Quaker=

Historie /

Von deren Ursprung /
biß auf jüngsthin entstandene
Trennung;

Darinnen vornemlich von
den Hauptstiftern dieser Secte /
derselben Lehrsätzen / und anderen
ihres gleichen zu dieser Zeit auf=
gebrachten Lehren / erzehlet
wird.

Berlin /
bey Johann Michael Rüdigern.
1696.

Plate XLI.—Title-page to German edition of Croese's "Quakeriana."

# THE
# General History
## OF THE
# QUAKERS:

CONTAINING

The Lives, Tenents, Sufferings, Tryals, Speeches, and Letters

Of all the most

# Eminent Quakers,

Both Men and Women;

From the first Rise of that SECT, down to this present Time.

*Collected from Manuscripts*, &c.

*A Work never attempted before in* English.

Being Written Originally in *Latin* By GERARD CROESE.

To which is added,

A LETTER writ by *George Keith*, and sent by him to the Author of this Book: Containing a Vindication of himself, and several Remarks on this History.

*LONDON*, Printed for John Dunton, at the *Raven* in *Jewen-street*. 1696.

Plate XLII.—Title-page of English edition of Croese's "Quakeriana."

RICHARDI BLOME
**Englisches**
AMERICA,
oder
Kurtze doch deutliche
**Beschreibung aller derer**
jenigen Länder und Inseln
so der Cron Engeland in West-In-
dien ietziger Zeit zuständig und
unterthänig sind.
durch eine hochberühmte Feder
aus dem Englischen übersetzt
und mit Kupffern gezieret.

(o)

Leipzig,
Bey Johann Großens Wittbe und Erben.
Anno. 1 6 9 7.

Plate XLIII.—Title-page to German edition of Blome's "English America." [From original in Carter Brown Library.]

# Ein

# Send-Brieff

### Offenhertziger Liebsbezeugung an die so genannte Pietisten in Hoch-Teutschland.

Zu AMSTERDAM,
Gedruckt vor Jacob Claus Buchhändler / 1697.

**Plate XLIV.**—Title-page of Pastorius' "Missive to the Pietists in Germany."

Henry Bernhard Koster, William Davis,
Thomas Rutter & Thomas Boryer,
FOUR
Boasting Disputers
Of this World briefly
REBUKED,
And Answered according to their Folly,
which they themselves have manifested in a
late Pamphlet, entituled, *Advice for all Pro-
fessors and Writers.*

By

*Francis Daniel Pastorius.*

Printed and Sold by *William Bradford* at the
Bible in *New-York,* 1697.

Plate XLV.—Title-page of Pastorius' "Rebuke."

An Hiſtorical and Geographical Account
OF THE
PROVINCE and COUNTRY
OF
PENSILVANIA;
AND OF
*Weſt-New-Jerſey*
IN
AMERICA.

The Richneſs of the Soil, the Sweetneſs of the Situation the Wholeſomneſs of the Air, the Navigable Rivers, and others, the prodigious Encreaſe of Corn, the flouriſhing Condition of the City of *Philadelphia*, with the ſtately Buildings, and other Improvements there. The ſtrange Creatures, as *Birds, Beaſts, Fiſhes,* and *Fowls,* with the ſeveral ſorts of *Minerals, Purging Waters,* and *Stones,* lately diſcovered. The *Natives, Aborogmes,* their Language, Religion, Laws, and *Cuſtoms*; The firſt Planters, the *Dutch, Sweeds,* and *Engliſh,* with the number of its Inhabitants; As alſo a Touch upon *George Keith's* New Religion, in his ſecond Change ſince he left the QUAKERS.

With a Map of both Countries.

By GABRIEL THOMAS,
who reſided there about Fifteen Years.

*London,* Printed for, and Sold by *A. Baldwin,* at the *Oxon Arms* in *Warwick-Lane,* 1698.

Plate XLVI.—Title-page of original edition of Gabriel Thomas' "Account."

# Die
# HISTORIA
## von
# PENSYLVANIA.

Enſylvania liegt zwiſchen der Breite des 40. und 45. Grades: Hat Weſt-Jerſey gegen Oſten / Virginien gegen Weſten / Marienland gegen Süden / und Canada gegen Norden. In der Länge hat es drey hundert / und in der Breite hundert und achzig Meilen.

Die in dem Land zu erſt gebohrne Völcker / oder erſte Einwohner dieſes Landes/werden/nach ihrem Urſprung/ bey den meiſten Völckern dafür gehalten / daß ſie von den zehen zerſtreueten Stämmen geweſen / weil ſie den Juden an der gantzen Geſtalt ſehr ähnlich ſind: Sie halten die Neu-Monde: ſie opffern ihre Erſtlinge einem / den ſie für einen Gott halten/ und Manito nennen/ deren ſie zwey haben / einen /( wie ſie ihnen einbilden) der oben wohnet und gut iſt / und einen andern/ der hier unten / und böß iſt / Dabey ſie eine Art von Lauberhütten. Jetzt ha-

Plate XLVII.—Heading of German edition of Gabriel Thomas' "Account."

Umständige Geographische

# Beschreibung

Der zu allerletzt erfundenen

## Proviñtz

# PENSYLVA-
## NIÆ,

In denen End-Gräntzen
### AMERICÆ
In der West-Welt gelegen/
Durch
### FRANCISCUM DANIELEM
PASTORIUM,
J. V. Lic. und Friedens-Richtern
daselbsten.

Worbey angehencket sind einige notable Begebenheiten / und Bericht-Schreiben an dessen Herrn Vattern
MELCHIOREM ADAMUM PASTO-
RIUM.
Und andere gute Freunde.

Franckfurt und Leipzig/
Zufinden bey Andreas Otto. 1700.

Plate XLVIII.—Title-page of Pastorius' "Geographical Description."
[First edition.]

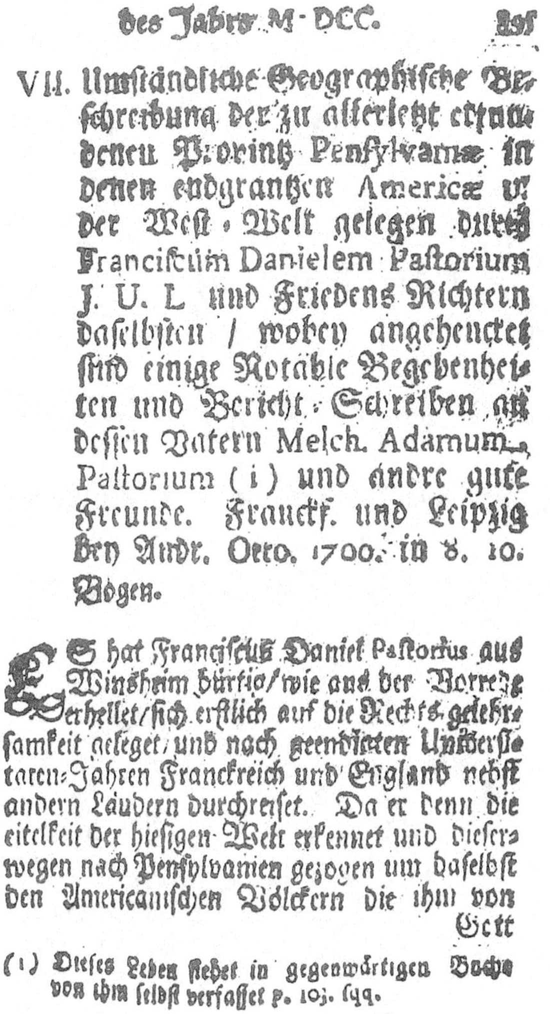

des Jahrs M · DCC.

VII. Umständliche Geographische Beschreibung der zu allerletzt erfundenen Proving Pensylvaniæ in denen endgrantzen Americæ u. der West-Welt gelegen durch Franciscum Danielem Pastorium J. U. L und Friedens Richtern daselbsten / wobey angehencket sind einige Notable Begebenheiten und Bericht-Schreiben an dessen Vatern Melch. Adamum. Pastorium (1) und andre gute Freunde. Franckf. und Leipzig bey Andr. Otto. 1700. in 8. 10. Bogen.

ES hat Franciscus Daniel Pastorius aus Winsheim bürtig/ wie aus der Vorrede erhellet/ sich erstlich auf die Rechtsgelehrsamkeit geleget/ und nach geendigten Universitaten-Jahren Franckreich und Engeland nebst andern Läudern durchreiset. Da er denn die eitelkeit der hiesigen Welt erkennet und dieserwegen nach Pensylvanien gezogen um daselbst den Americanischen Völckern die ihm von
Gott

(1) Dieses Leben stehet in gegenwärtigen Buche von ihm selbst verfasset p. 103. sqq.

Plate XLIX.—Heading from Pastorius' Description in *Monathlicher Auszug*. Hanover, 1700.

# BRIEF

Aan den

## KONING van POOLEN.

Opgestelt door

## WILLIAM PENN,

*Uyt de Naam van zijn verdrukte en lydende Vrienden*
tot D A N T Z I G.

Uit het Engelsch vertaald

D O O R

P. V. M.

t'A M S T E L D A M,
By J A C O B C L A U S,
Boekverkoper in de Prince-straat. 1701.

Plate L.—Title-page of Penn's "Missive to the King of Poland."
[From the original in Carter Brown Library.]

# Curieuse Nachricht
## Von
# PENSYLVANIA
### in
# Norden-America

Welche /
Auf Begehren guter Freunde/
Über vorgelegte 103. Fragen/ bey seiner Abreiß aus Teutschland nach obigem Lande Anno 1700.
ertheilet/ und nun Anno 1702 in den Druck
gegeben worden.
Von
**Daniel Falknern/** Professore,
Burgern und Pilgrim allda.

Franckfurt und Leipzig /
Zu finden bey Andreas Otto/ Buchhändlern.
Im Jahr Christi 1702.

**Plate LI.**—Title-page of Falkner's "Curious Information."
[From Diffenderffer's "Great Exodus to England."]

# Abdruck Eines Schreibens

## An
### Tit. Herrn
# D. Henr. Muhlen/

**Aus Germanton/ in der Americanischen** Province Penſylvania, ſonſt Nova Suecia, den erſten Auguſti, im Jahr unſers Heyls eintauſend ſiebenhundert und eins,

### Den Zuſtand der Kirchen in America betreffend.

MDCCII.

---

**Plate LII.**—Title-page of Justus Falckner's "Account of the Religious Condition in America." [From the original in the University of Rostock, Germany.]

# Quäcker-Greuel,

Das ist:

**Abscheuliche/ auffrührische/ verdammliche Irrthum**

## Der neuen Schwermer,

Welche genennet werden

## Quäcker,

Wie sie dieselbe in ihren Scartecken/ Allarm/ Standarte/ Pannier/ Königreich/ Eckstein/ und sonst schrifftlich und mündlich mit grossem Ergerniß ausgebreitet.

Auf Anordnung Eines Edlen Hochweisen Raths

### Der Stadt Hamburg

Den Einfältigen zu treuhertziger Warnung kurtzlich gefasset/ gründlich widerleget/ und in Druck gegeben

durch

Etliche hierzu verordnete

Des Ministerii in Hamburg.

Auf Begehren hoher Personen auffs neue gedruckt
Im Jahr Christi 1702.

**Plate LIII.**—Title-page of a specimen of "Anti-Quakeriana."

Umständige Geographische
**Beschreibung**
Der zu allerletzt erfundenen
**Provintz**
PENSYLVA-
NIÆ,
In denen End-Gräntzen
AMERICÆ
In der West-Welt gelegen,
Durch
FRANCISCUM DANIELEM
PASTORIUM,
J. V. Lic. und Friedens-Richtern
daselbsten.

Worbey angehencket sind einige no-
table Begebenheiten/ und Bericht-
Schreiben an dessen Herrn
Vattern
MELCHIOREM ADAMUM
PASTORIUM,
Und andere gute Freunde.

Franckfurt und Leipzig/
Zufinden bey Andreas Otto. 1704.

Plate LIV.—Title-page of second edition of Pastorius' "Geographical Description."

[From Diffenderffer's "Great Exodus to England."]

# CONTINUATIO
Der
Beschreibung der Landschafft
## PENSYLVANIÆ
An denen End-Gräntzen
## AMERICÆ.
Uber vorige des Herrn Pastorii
Relationes.
In sich haltend:
Die Situation, und Fruchtbarkeit des
Erdbodens. Die Schiffreiche und andere
Flüsse. Die Anzahl derer bißhero gebauten Städte.
Die seltsame Creaturen an Thieren/ Vögeln und Fischen.
Die Mineralien und Edelgesteine Deren eingebohrnen wilden Völcker Sprachen/ Religion und Gebräuche. Und
die ersten Christlichen Pflantzer und Anbauer
dieses Landes.

Beschrieben von
## GABRIEL THOMAS
15. Jährigen Inwohner dieses
Landes.

Welchem Tractätlein noch beygefüget sind:
Des Hn. DANIEL FALCKNERS
Burgers und Pilgrims in Pensylvania 193.
Beantwortungen uff vorgelegte Fragen von
guten Freunden.

Franckfurt und Leipzig/
Zu finden bey Andreas Otto/ Buchhändlern.

Plate LV.—Title-page of Pastorius' "Continuation."
[From Diffenderffer's "Great Exodus to England."]

DISSERTATIO HISTORICO-THEOLOGICA
DE
# PHILTRIS
## ENTHUSIASTICIS AN-GLICO BATAVIS
H. E.
**Von dem Englisch-und Holländischen Quaker-Pulver**

QVAM
CONSENTIENTE SUMME REVER. FACULTATE THEOLOGICA
SUB MAGNIFICO RECTORALI ATQVE DECANALI
MODERAMINE

## GRAPIANO
### PRÆSIDE

VIRO PLURIMUM REVERENDO, NOBILISSIMO, ATQVE PRÆ-
CELLENTISSIMO,

## DN. PETRO ZORNIO,
BONARUM ARTIUM MAGISTRO DEXTERRIMO, S. S. THEOLOGIÆ
BACCALAUREO CELEBERRIMO DIGNISSIMOQVE,
DN. FAUTORE AC PROMOTORE STU-
DIORUM SUORUM ÆTERNUM COLENDO
D. XIX. JAN. ANNO MDCCVII.
IN AUDITORIO MAXIMO
Horis consvetis
PUBLICÆ PLACIDÆQVE ERUDITORUM DISQVISITIONI SISTIT

## JOH. PHIL. SA-WART.
LUNEBURGENSIS. S. S. Theol. Stud.

Rostochi, Typis Joh. Wepplingi, SEREN. PRINC. & ACAD. Typog.

Plate LVI.—Specimen of "Anti-Quakeriana."

# PART THREE - EDITOR'S CONCLUSION

## CONCLUSION

As noted in the Preface, 1992 marks an important date in world history - the discovery/re-discovery of America. The purpose of this volume has been to demonstrate the German role in the discovery, exploration, and settlement of the New World. The German involvement is underscored by the fact that Germans have constituted the largest single immigrant group which has come to America in the last five centuries. It is, therefore, not altogether surprising that German-Americans make up the largest single ethnic element in the U.S., according to the U.S. Census.

In the course of the last five centuries, America, in a very real sense, became the frontier of Europe, especially for the German-speaking countries which sent millions westward. The roots of these interrelationships are to be found with the discovery of America in the fifteenth century.

Today, as America stands on the threshold of a new century, the great immigration waves are over, but an examination of their beginnings helps us understand not only how they came about, but how they all ultimately emanate from the discovery in 1492. Moreover, they demonstrate the interrelatedness of the Old and the New Worlds. Furthermore, these Old and New World connections and associations continue to be as important and vital today - socially, economicially, politically, and culturally.

One of the major strands in the Old/New World relationship is the German-American connection, especially as millions of German-Americans explore their German roots, and the overall history of the relationships between Germany and the U.S. An excellent starting point for an exploration of these various cross-cultural interrelationships is to be found at the very beginning of German-American contacts.

For those interested in further detailed exploration of these topics, the editor has included a number of relevant works, which the reader may want to consult.

Sources for Further Reading:

1. Bibliographies of German-American history

There are several basic bibliographies which the reader should consult for more in-depth references to the various aspects of German-American history. For materials published before 1940, see Henry A. Pochmann, *Bibliography of German Culture in America to 1940* (1953). For materials published after 1940, see Don Heinrich Tolzmann, *German-Americana: A Bibliography* (1975). For a more in-depth and annotated bibliography which covers both time-periods, see Don Heinrich Tolzmann, *Catalog of the German-Americana Collection, University of Cincinnati* (1990). In these reference works, the reader will find comprehensive listings of the primary and secondary sources pertaining to the history of German immigration and settlement in the U.S.

2. General Histories of the German Element in the U.S.

The standard history of German-Americans is Albert B. Faust, *The German Element in the U.S.* (1927), which is now, unfortunately, quite out-of-date, but is still the basic source for the period before the First World War. Other general histories are: Robert H. Billigmeier, *Americans from Germany: A Study in Cultural Diversity* (1974); Dieter Cunz, *They Came from Germany: The Stories of Famous German-Americans* (1966); Howard B. Furer, *The Germans in America, 1607-1970: A Chronology and Fact Book* (1973); Richard O'Connor, *The German-Americans* (1968); Joseph Wandel, *The German Dimension in American History* (1979); and Klaus Wust, *Three Hundred Years of German Immigrants in North America* (1983). The best one-volume general history in print is LaVern J. Rippley, *The German-Americans* (1976).

3. Histories of Germany

Among the many histories of Germany, a good starting place is Geoffrey Barraclough, *The Origins of Modern Germany* (1947), which is indispensable for an understanding of the origins of modern Germany. Another valuable and basic history is Hajo Holborn, *A History of Modern Germany* (1959-69), a work which begins with the Reformation and brings German history up to the recent past.

## 4. Histories of German-American Relations

For those interested in a history of the relationships between Germany and America, the reader should consult Thomas Piltz, *Die Deutschen und die Amerikaner/The Americans and the Germans* (1977) and Wolfgang Glaser, *Americans and Germans: A Handy Reader and Reference Book/Deutsche und Amerikaner: Ein Lese- und Nachschlagebuch* (1986). Also useful are the following works: Thomas Piltz, *Aspects of German-American Relations in History, Politics, Economics and Culture* (1986) and Heinz Moos, *America: The New Canaan/Amerika als neues Kanaan* (1987). The earliest political relationships are documented in Karl J.R. Arndt, *The Treaty of Amity and Commerce of 1785 between his Majesty the King of Prussia and the United States of America/Der Freundschafts- und Handelsvertrag von 1786 zwischen Seiner Majestaet dem Koenig von Preussen und den Vereinigten Staaten von Amerika* (1977).

## 5. Special Anniversary Histories

In 1893 a well known German-American historian published a history of America in commemoration of the 400th anniversary of the discovery of America: G.A. Zimmermann, *Vierhundert Jahre Amerikanischer Geschichte: Zur 400jaehrigen Jubelfeier der Entdeckung von Amerika* (1893). In 1991-92 Don Heinrich Tolzmann published two volumes, one in English and one in German, for the five-hundredth anniversary of the discovery of America, the first being this volume, and the second, *In der Neuen Welt: Deutsch-Amerikanische Festschrift fuer die 500-Jahrfeier der Entdeckung von Amerika* (1992).

Works by the Editor:

*German-Americana: A Bibliography* (1975)

*America's German Heritage* (1976)

*German-American Literature* (1977)

*Festschrift for the German-American Tricentennial Jubilee: Cincinnati 1983* (1982)

*The Cincinnati Germans after the Great War* (1987)

*The First Description of Cincinnati and other Ohio Settlements: The Travel Report of Johann Heckewelder, 1792* (1988)

*Spring Grove and its Creator: H.A. Rattermann's Biography of Adolph Strauch* (1988)

*Catalog of the German-Americana Collection, University of Cincinnati* (1990)

*The First Mayor of Cincinnati: George A. Katzenberger's Biography of Major David Ziegler* (1990)

*New German-American Studies* (1990- )

*Germany and America (1450-1700): Julius Friedrich Sachse's History of the German Role in the Discovery, Exploration and Settlement of the New World* (1991)

*In 'der Neuen Heimat: Deutsch-Amerikanische Festschrift fuer die 500-Jahrfeier der Entdeckung von Amerika* (1992)

www.ingramcontent.com/pod-product-compliance
Lightning Source LLC
Chambersburg PA
CBHW060554230426
43670CB00011B/1816